Introduction

Contemporary fashion is motivated by continual change and new ideas. Fuelling this process is a diverse group of radical new designers who are questioning the current style zeitgeist and rapidly propelling fashion forward.

100 New Fashion Designers is an international snapshot of modern fashion design and those individuals who play an integral role in it. This new generation of designers is defined by an eagerness to present a unique and personal philosophy of clothing and fashion design. Encompassing menswear, womenswear and accessories design, the fashion industry is no longer confined by style rules or traditional manufacturing processes and methods, but is firmly focused on the sole expression of designers' individuality, creativity and vision.

Fashion now exists in a global community where images of the latest catwalk shows are available to everyone online, and if you own a credit card you can purchase anything from anywhere. While fashion may have lost some of its previous mystique, it is still a global industry that fascinates consumers, enthrals spectators and continually grows in to an increasingly powerful and significant part of our lives.

However, to the new designers featured here, the globalization of fashion and the power of big brands are at the opposite end of the fashion spectrum in terms of what they are trying to achieve. Instead of mass market appeal and homogenization of fashion, these creatives are focused on developing their own singular vision and reinterpreting contemporary clothing. Their work is not all about developing big business and selling huge quantities of clothes, but is concerned with suggesting new concepts and tapping in to a consumer desire for alternatives in fashion.

New fashion designers, although distinct in their own aesthetic and design sensibilities, are all linked in their determination to present an individual interpretation of clothing design. While informed by their own particular environments and educational backgrounds, the designers included in this book are as diverse as they are gloriously radical.

100 New Fashion Designers attempts to capture the current zeitgeist, those key moments in fashion that are defined and redefined by the creative designers who work within this ever changing field. As fashion seasons are transient, this book helps to identify the prevalent aesthetic that the featured designers have established as their own signature style.

The foundations for many of these creative designers are the international fashion colleges and institutions that support and nurture this wealth of talent. In New York, Parsons the New School for Design and the Fashion Institute of Technology (FIT) both produce graduates that balance a commercial sensibility with new ideas. In Belgium The Royal Academy of Fine Arts in Antwerp has a reputation for unrivalled creativity, while Bunka Fashion College in Tokyo is renowned for providing students with a wealth of technical knowledge.

Ultimately, London's Central Saint Martins and The Royal College of Art are the world leaders in producing the best new talent in fashion design. Both with a focus on supporting and developing students' new ideas and creativity, these two colleges are intrinsic in the success of new international fashion talent. While this book features designers from all over the world, the majority of them have studied and have their roots at these esteemed London colleges.

As London hosts the most revered fashion colleges, it is natural that the city has become a platform for supporting new talent. London provides new designers with the opportunity to showcase their work like no other capital. 'I think it is commonly accepted now that UK fashion universities produce the best designers in the world, and this is reflected in the amount of British talent which can be found in key positions in international design houses', explains Terry Mansfield, chairman of London's Graduate Fashion Week which was set up in 1991 to create a London-based event with both a static exhibition and professional catwalk shows for UK fashion design colleges. 'That's what makes Graduate Fashion Week exciting', believes Mansfield, 'it really is the place to spot the next big thing.'

London is also fortunate to be supported by fashion initiatives that promote new designers after they have left college. Vauxhall Fashion Scout, Fashion Forward, New Generation, On/Off and Blow's Off Schedule guide have all been established with a view to strengthening and promoting new fashion talent.

One of the first of these initiatives was The Old Truman Brewery in London's East End, which set up Fashion East to help young designers break through at London Fashion Week. The initiative assists new designers in producing runway shows, sourcing sponsorship and promoting their work. Recent designers who have benefited from their support include *PPQ, Jens Laugesen, Jonathan Saunders, Richard Nicoll, Spijkers en Spijkers, Meadham/Kirchhoff, Danielle Scutt, Siv Støldal, Deryck Walker, Patrik Söderstam, Cassette Playa* and *Carola Euler.*

UK fashion chain Topshop have sponsored the womenswear show since 2003, and Topman have sponsored the menswear show, 'MAN', since 2005. A panel of journalists, stylists, buyers and other established designers select the participating designers. 'Our decision is quite intuitive', explains founder Lulu Kennedy, 'It's hard to pinpoint what we look for, but we know it when we see it. The main thing is it must feel fresh and directional.'

Kennedy admits that London's great success in supporting new designers may lead to saturation: 'If too many organizations support designers it will lead to that. I am only interested in those designers that I feel are genuinely talented and relevant, and if there's a lack of good designers I'd rather have a season off than compromise and work with a second rate designer.'

On a global scale ITS (International Talent Support) fashion competition was set up by EVE, an agency based in Trieste, Italy. The event began with a fashion competition for young new designers, thus answering the needs of both the fashion industry and schools at an international level. Due to the success of the competition, photography and accessories are also now represented at the event, which is funded by its main partners Diesel, YKK and MINI. 'We look for the best in creativity and beauty, which is of course not restricted by any given nationality', explains ITS events director Barbara Franchin.

'This is something that makes ITS unique. While there are many national competitions that select finalists of all nationalities that are based and study in Europe, ITS hosts around 20 fashion designers a year, representing a wider spectrum of what is going on in the world.' *Cathy Pill,* Marcus Wilmont from *Aminaka Wilmont, Heather Blake, Aitor Throup, Natalia Brilli, Slobodan Mihajlovic* and *Peter Pilotto* have all launched their careers at ITS.

Although it has an international focus, ITS still sees the best entries coming from particular colleges: 'from the UK, Central Saint Martins and The Royal College of Art, and from The Royal Academy of Fine Art in Belgium – these three schools guarantee a high level of creativity and quality. Although every year there are surprises from unexpected countries that happily compete with the more conventional fashion countries', says Franchin.

Aside from these fashion competitions, London also has a fantastic network of fashion public relations companies that support emerging talent. Notably Mandi Lennard Publicity and Michael Oliver-Salac of Blow PR provide very important access platforms for international press and buyers, which is essential for those wanting to see London's newest talent.

100 New Fashion Designers **features those** designers who have, since the millennium, presented a new vision for fashion. All with a focus on innovation and new ideas, they have taken the fundamental elements of fashion – colour, silhouette, proportion and fabric – and revolutionized the way we think about clothes.

From the mavericks to the mainstream, from celebrities to club kids, everyone is interested in fashion. And, while fashion and style has high currency, ever more concerned with ethical issues surrounding cheap t-shirts and the extravagances of high couture, it seems that all of us still have a thirst for the new.

In defining the future of fashion these designers represent innovation and creative expression, and it is through their visionary endeavours and experimentation that the fashion world is constantly progressive and contemporary. In an industry that reveres new talent this book uncovers just 100 of the radical new designers who are each fulfilling important individual roles as innovators.

1

2

3

*****L is a concept-driven, subversive streetwear label based on a reversed luxury lifestyle concept. Created by Thierry Le Pin, former head of design and production at Joseph and sales executive at Yohji Yamamoto, the brand is built on an idealized yet ironic idea of the luxury hotel.

*****L____1/100

The label's name stands for *'Cinq Étoiles Luxe'* (five-star luxury), referring to the international system of hotel classification. Along with garments, the label produces a range of products and accessories closely associated with opulent hotel style, including a home collection, bath range, luggage and fine stationery, and turns the luxury hotel symbol into a global lifestyle brand.

One of *****L's aims is to break the fashion cliché that a high-quality product equals a high price tag. The staple material used is a custom-made cotton velour fabric that is both durable and decadent. Subtle touches, such as old-fashioned woven washing tags, decorative zippers and accompanying custom-designed shopping bags, set the products apart from mass-produced streetwear brands.

Although the clothing range was initially designed as menswear, the lean-proportioned garments are also suited to women. The label's original and iconic white jersey velvet and gold-star-emblazoned jogging suits are inspired by the elusive yet familiar fantasy of extravagant hotel living, turning stuffy symbols of wealth and excess into cool and affordable streetwear. *****L also comments on society's obsession with brand names. It is the first label outside fashion conglomerates and worldwide designer brands to explore the concept of lifestyle environment.

Describe your design philosophy. *Room service.*

How would you define your aesthetic? *Sportswear meets luxury. Luxury meets sportswear.*

What is the most enjoyable part of design? *Mixing codes.*

How would you describe your creative process? *Getting the right balance between fabrics, details and production.*

How would you define contemporary fashion? *It's all about industry.*

Who or what informs your work? *Traditions, streets, sports.*

What is the most challenging aspect of design? *Making things happen.*

www.cinqetoilesluxe.com

1. Brights from S/S 08 Lookbook. 2. Boxing bathrobe, A/W 03. 3. 100% silk grey marl casual vest, S/S 03. 4–6. Cotton velour sweater; hooded sweatshirt; padded jacket. All A/W 07. 7. Camel velour sweatsuit, S/S 03. 8. Cotton hoody and casual zip tops, A/W 03. 9. Cotton vests and leggings, S/S 03.

'Sportswear meets luxury.
Luxury meets sportswear.'
—— *****L

7

8

9

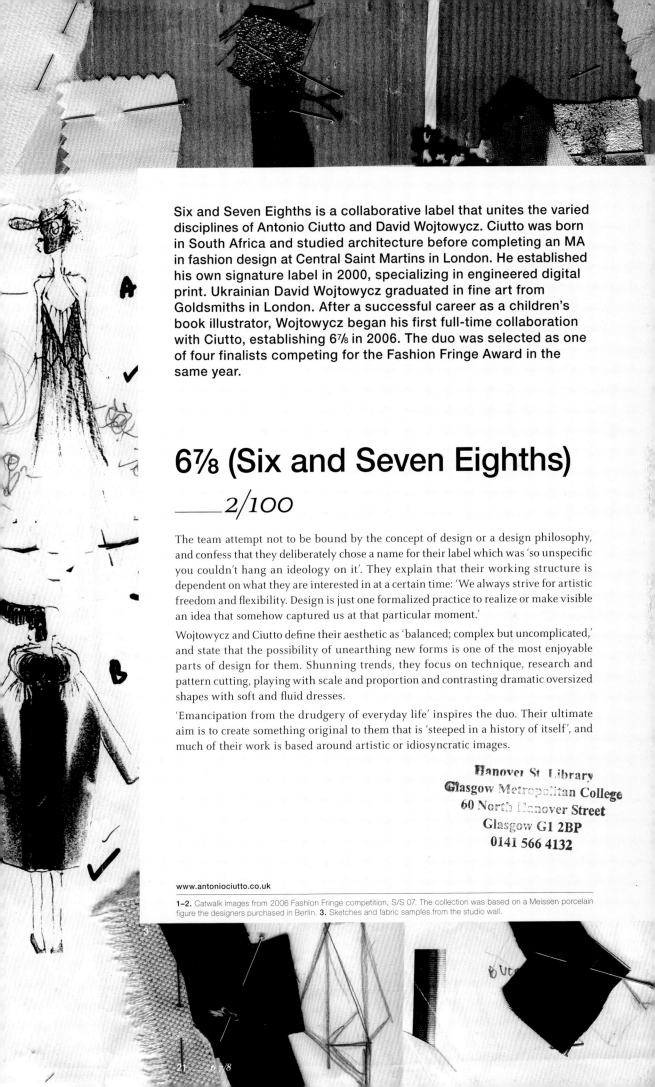

Six and Seven Eighths is a collaborative label that unites the varied disciplines of Antonio Ciutto and David Wojtowycz. Ciutto was born in South Africa and studied architecture before completing an MA in fashion design at Central Saint Martins in London. He established his own signature label in 2000, specializing in engineered digital print. Ukrainian David Wojtowycz graduated in fine art from Goldsmiths in London. After a successful career as a children's book illustrator, Wojtowycz began his first full-time collaboration with Ciutto, establishing 6⅞ in 2006. The duo was selected as one of four finalists competing for the Fashion Fringe Award in the same year.

6⅞ (Six and Seven Eighths)
___2/100

The team attempt not to be bound by the concept of design or a design philosophy, and confess that they deliberately chose a name for their label which was 'so unspecific you couldn't hang an ideology on it'. They explain that their working structure is dependent on what they are interested in at a certain time: 'We always strive for artistic freedom and flexibility. Design is just one formalized practice to realize or make visible an idea that somehow captured us at that particular moment.'

Wojtowycz and Ciutto define their aesthetic as 'balanced; complex but uncomplicated,' and state that the possibility of unearthing new forms is one of the most enjoyable parts of design for them. Shunning trends, they focus on technique, research and pattern cutting, playing with scale and proportion and contrasting dramatic oversized shapes with soft and fluid dresses.

'Emancipation from the drudgery of everyday life' inspires the duo. Their ultimate aim is to create something original to them that is 'steeped in a history of itself', and much of their work is based around artistic or idiosyncratic images.

www.antoniociutto.co.uk

1–2. Catwalk images from 2006 Fashion Fringe competition, S/S 07. The collection was based on a Meissen porcelain figure the designers purchased in Berlin. **3.** Sketches and fabric samples from the studio wall.

21 — 6⅞

1

2

Seiichiro Shimamura is the creative art director behind the label 0044. Working in advertising, Shimamura was attracted to the beauty of Paris and decided to open an atelier in 1996. The following year he opened a store in the Harajuku area of Tokyo, called 'no44', which became influential for its mix of European vintage clothing, designer collections and its own-name original line. To fulfil his concept in 2003, Shimamura created both men's and women's collections, called '0044 Paris', and his first store opened in Paris in 2005.

0044____3/100

Every garment begins life in the designer's imagination, sometimes inspired by a short film or even a poem. The essence of the story is then developed and transformed into the shape of clothes or accessories. Describing his design philosophy as 'Revolutionary Romanticism', Shimamura explains that he aims 'to respect the intuition and the feelings and free imagination and to find the balance between the creativity and the destruction.'

During the process of design Shimamura thrives. 'Each of our collections is based on a narrative. I enjoy the creative process of making up a story, which is often a spontaneous process that is composed of intelligence and sensibility. To find the basic principles of life itself is challenging but what is even more challenging is to express them through fashion as our message to the world.'

People in the creative fields – cinema, theatre, music and architecture – are all drawn to the collections. 'Contemporary fashion should be simple and minimal and yet suggest the beauty and freshness of a time,' states Shimamura, who finds it a challenge to be creative consistently and to have the courage to believe in himself. 'We try to create 0044's own standard of beauty aggressively and sensitively,' he says. 'We send our messages by expressing our world not only through our clothing collections, but also through all other creations.'

www.0044paris.com

1. Black-dyed US flag from S/S 08 show. 2. Waistcoat made from vintage jacquard drapes, S/S 06. 3. Concept sketches, S/S 07. 4. Cotton bondage t-shirt, A/W 07. 5–8. Hat made from US flag, jacket made from British army scarf, S/S 08. 9. Cotton and viscose swallow-tail waistcoat, S/S 06. 10. First official catwalk show for 0044 Paris, S/S 07. 11. Flared, hooded sweatshirt, S/S 08.

3

'Contemporary fashion should be simple and minimal and yet suggest the beauty and freshness of a time' **0044**

1

2

'Eccentric but with a classical perspective' describes Aimee McWilliams's signature aesthetic. An accomplished designer, illustrator and stylist, she represents the progressive attitude of the new wave of British designers.

Aimee McWilliams___*4/100*

McWilliams graduated from Central Saint Martins in London in 2003. In the same year, her collection, entitled 'Sub Couture', won the L'Oreal Total Look Award, and the following year she launched her own label. After working closely with top designers, including Stella McCartney, Rachel Lopez and Alexander McQueen, she debuted her Autumn/Winter collection at London Fashion Week in 2004.

Firmly establishing her contemporary aesthetic, McWilliams focuses on an avant-garde approach to design and pattern cutting. She works with diverse fabrics, from heavy fur through to fluid chiffon, and also uses print and embroidery in her collections.

Describing her approach to design as a philosophy, McWilliams explains, 'My designs are a result of my willingness to acknowledge everything that I am attracted to'. Integral to this design process is intensive research, which leads to a body of information and inspiration that evolves with every season. Each collection begins with the development of a 3D collage illustration that informs the design concept. McWilliams describes these collages as 'my bible for the season, whether I'm designing a collection or directing a shoot, they are a constant source of inspiration'.

The designer recognizes that her clients are often strong and directional in character and appearance, and perhaps even a little eccentric by nature. She finds the most challenging aspect of design is pushing herself to innovate at every stage of the process and to reflect continuously to ensure she is meeting her goals and objectives.

McWilliams has also worked as a stylist for the Rolling Stones, who commissioned her to create showpieces for their world tours, and in 2006 she was awarded the Scottish Designer of the Year title.

www.aimeemcwilliams.com

1. Belted suit with grown-on gloves, A/W 06. 2. Oversized angora knit and black patent leather trousers, A/W 06. 3–4. Collage artwork, A/W 06. 5. Buckle-detail trousers with classic black jersey top and Garbo gloves, A/W 06. 6. Collage artwork, A/W 06.

'My designs are a result of my willingness to acknowledge everything that I am attracted to _____Aimee McWilliams

3

4

5

6

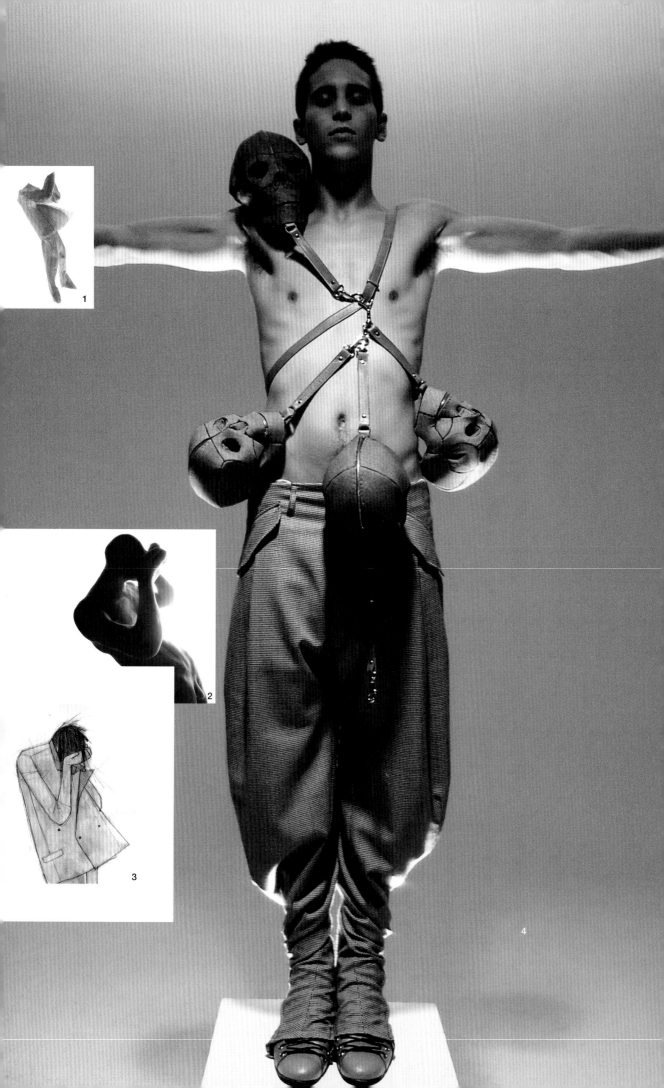

1

2

3

4

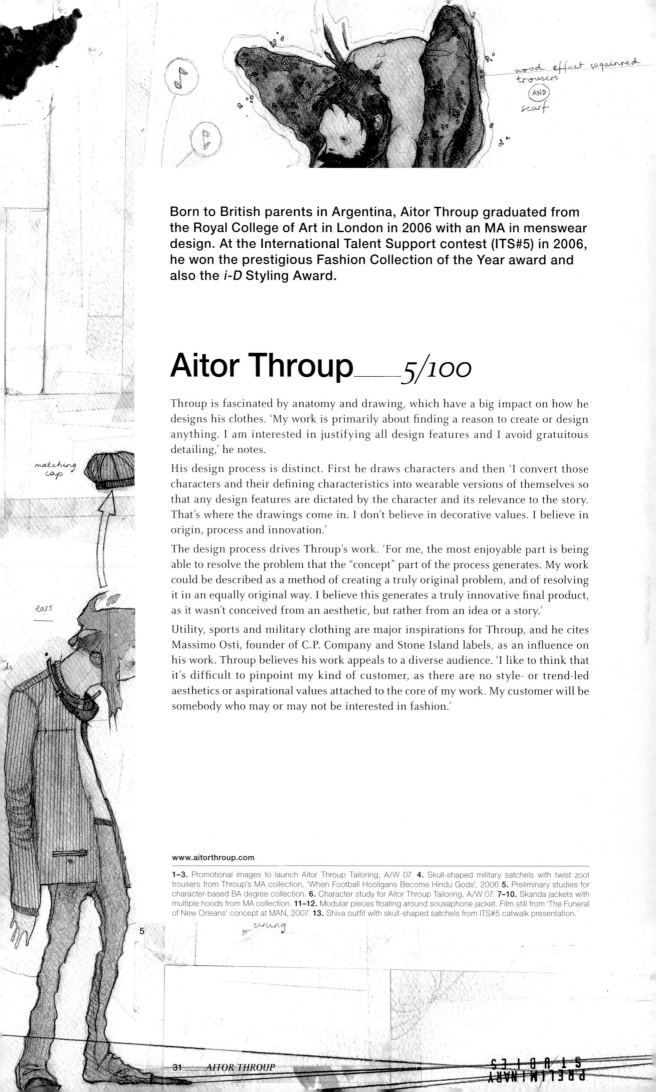

wood effect sequinned
trousers
AND
scarf

Born to British parents in Argentina, Aitor Throup graduated from the Royal College of Art in London in 2006 with an MA in menswear design. At the International Talent Support contest (ITS#5) in 2006, he won the prestigious Fashion Collection of the Year award and also the *i-D* Styling Award.

matching
cap

Aitor Throup___5/100

Throup is fascinated by anatomy and drawing, which have a big impact on how he designs his clothes. 'My work is primarily about finding a reason to create or design anything. I am interested in justifying all design features and I avoid gratuitous detailing,' he notes.

His design process is distinct. First he draws characters and then 'I convert those characters and their defining characteristics into wearable versions of themselves so that any design features are dictated by the character and its relevance to the story. That's where the drawings come in. I don't believe in decorative values. I believe in origin, process and innovation.'

The design process drives Throup's work. 'For me, the most enjoyable part is being able to resolve the problem that the "concept" part of the process generates. My work could be described as a method of creating a truly original problem, and of resolving it in an equally original way. I believe this generates a truly innovative final product, as it wasn't conceived from an aesthetic, but rather from an idea or a story.'

Utility, sports and military clothing are major inspirations for Throup, and he cites Massimo Osti, founder of C.P. Company and Stone Island labels, as an influence on his work. Throup believes his work appeals to a diverse audience. 'I like to think that it's difficult to pinpoint my kind of customer, as there are no style- or trend-led aesthetics or aspirational values attached to the core of my work. My customer will be somebody who may or may not be interested in fashion.'

ears

www.aitorthroup.com

1–3. Promotional images to launch Aitor Throup Tailoring, A/W 07. 4. Skull-shaped military satchels with twist zoot trousers from Throup's MA collection, 'When Football Hooligans Become Hindu Gods', 2006 5. Preliminary studies for character-based BA degree collection. 6. Character study for Aitor Throup Tailoring, A/W 07. 7–10. Skanda jackets with multiple hoods from MA collection. 11–12. Modular pieces floating around sousaphone jacket. Film still from 'The Funeral of New Orleans' concept at MAN, 2007. 13. Shiva outfit with skull-shaped satchels from ITS#5 catwalk presentation.

5

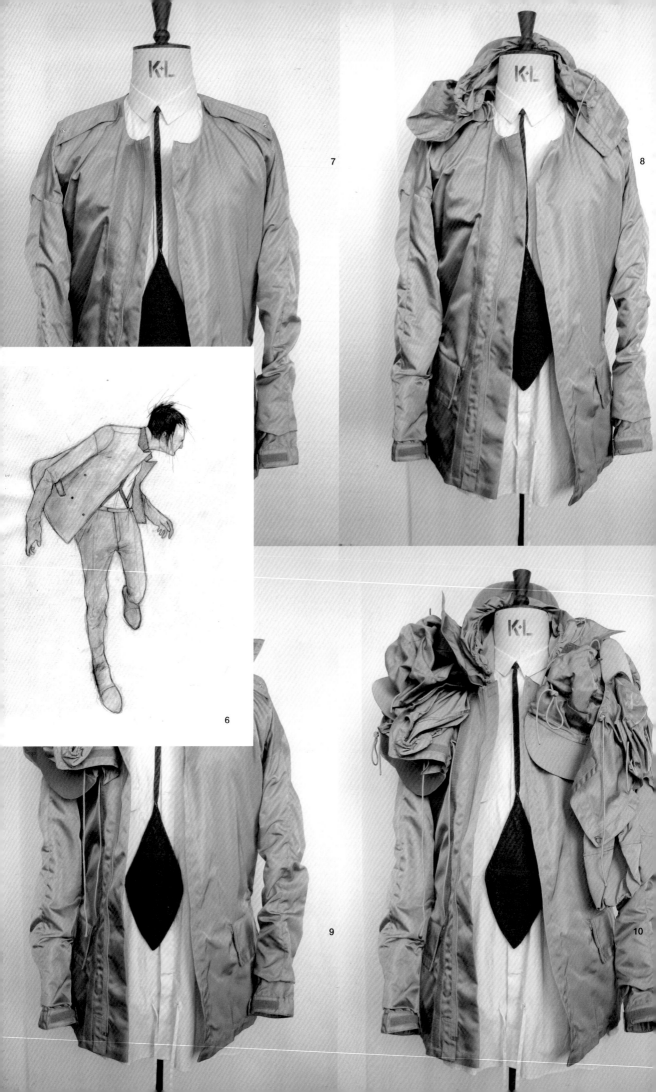

7

8

6

9

10

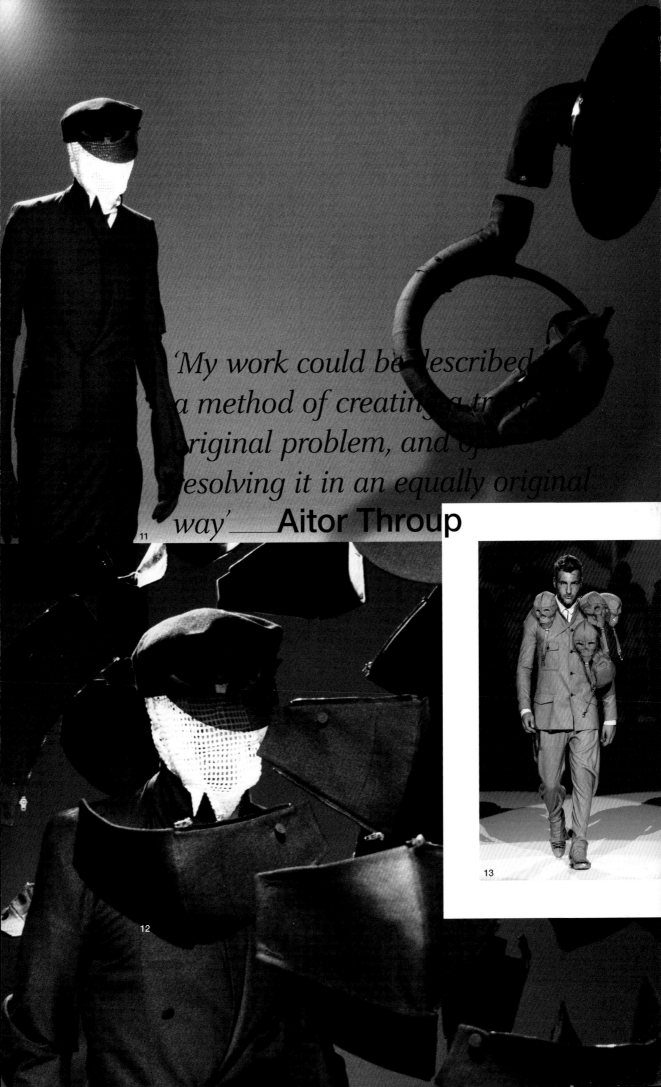

'My work could be described a method of creating tr original problem, and resolving it in an equally original way'___**Aitor Throup**

11

12

13

2

3

4

5

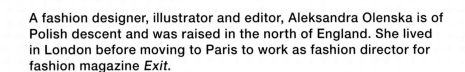

A fashion designer, illustrator and editor, Aleksandra Olenska is of Polish descent and was raised in the north of England. She lived in London before moving to Paris to work as fashion director for fashion magazine *Exit*.

Aleksandra Olenska___*6/100*

Olenska's career in fashion began when she worked for the influential fashion magazine *Dazed and Confused* in the mid 1990s. She then enrolled on the MA course at London's Central Saint Martins in 2003, where *her* innovative mix of styling, design and accessories came to the attention of *10* magazine, Italian *Vogue* and *Self Service Magazine*.

Since that time, her accessories have appeared on the catwalks of several international designers: she created a couture hosiery collection and accessories for Roksanda Ilincic in London for Autumn/Winter 04/05, she produced hosiery for Vanessa Bruno's Autumn/Winter 04/05 collection and produced shoes for Peter Jensen's Autumn/Winter 04/05 line. Olenska has also contributed prints to Clements Ribeiro's Spring/Summer 04 collection and to Hugo Boss's Autumn/Winter 04/05 line. Other collaborations have included creating accessories for Alistair Carr, Russell Sage and Megan Park. She has contributed to online interactive fashion and art project SHOWstudio, designed a shoe line for Topshop and created countless fashion editorials. Furthermore, as a stylist, Olenska's work has appeared in Japanese *Vogue, Tatler, Nylon, The Independent* and *Dazed and Confused*. Clements Ribeiro and Hugo Boss have both used Olenska's illustrations.

Olenska's Polish heritage informs her work. She describes her aesthetic: 'In 2004 scientists used a technique called germ-line transformation to cross a butterfly with a jellyfish, resulting in a glow-in-the-dark butterfly. A dash of an Eastern European Edith Sitwell tinged with melancholia.' Olenska is hopeful about the future of design and strives to do as she feels is right at any one moment. Her contribution to contemporary fashion through accessories and styling fashion images is proof that not only fashion designers make an impact on the industry.

www.aleksandraolenska.com

1. Brocade bathing suit made from vintage dresses worn with hand-appliquéd velvet, glove-leather tights and handpainted platform shoes. Shoot for *10* magazine. **2-5.** Jewelled glove-leather bow mask; shell and horsehair necklace, ruffle dot tights; appliqué tights; sycamore and Swarovski crystal necklace. All S/S 05. **6.** Design sketches for butterfly tights created for *10* magazine.

6

1

2

Russian Alena Akhmadullina studied at St. Petersburg State University of Technology and Design from 1995 to 2000. In 2000, she was a finalist in the Smirnoff Fashion Award competition in Moscow and was chosen to represent Russia at the Mittelmoda competition in Gorizia, Italy.

Alena Akhmadullina___7/100

Since 2001, Akhmadullina has been creating distinctive prêt-à-porter collections. Her debut Autumn/Winter 01/02 collection, entitled 'It Will Be So With Everyone', was presented at Russian Fashion Week and established the clean, concise silhouettes and exquisite proportions that now define her aesthetic. 'The craziest ideas and unexpected materials can be adapted for everyday life' became the motto of the young designer.

Many different periods of Russian culture inspire Akhmadullina, whose references span from the splendour of the courts of Russian Tsars to the constructivism of the 1920s and 1930s. 'I am not an artist who thinks with a pen in her hand,' she explains. 'Ideas occur in a sudden way. I put them into shelves of my mind's library, preserving a part of them, giving others time to mature, and realizing the rest of them immediately.'

Daring and avant-garde, the collections have created a phenomenon in Russian fashion. Described by the designer as 'bourgeois punk', the image of the collection is clear and contemporary. 'My customer is a highly independent, educated and confident woman. She wears our garments in order to compile her unique image. Women who dress in *Alena Akhmadullina* will always have a kind of mystery, inner accuracy and trustworthiness. And her clothes are conceptual, novel and well thought out,' explains Akhmadullina.

Contemporary fashion, according to Akhmadullina, is a fast-moving, complex, multi-layered business. 'Modern consumers require new goods to appear on the shelves approximately every two months and this is difficult for designers to produce.' Finding a balance between the commercial and the creative is also a key issue for Akhmadullina as she strives to make the very best contemporary clothes.

www.alenaakhmadullina.com

1. Knitted wool dress with imitation plaits and cotton pantaloons, A/W 07. 2. Printed cotton suit with imitation printed waistcoat and white cotton shirt, S/S 07. 3. Long layered cotton dress, S/S 07. 4. Knitted coat with imitation plaits and mink button-on collar and cotton jogging pants, A/W 07. 5. Voluminous white dress with bow details and headdress, S/S 07. 6. White jacket and pants, S/S 07. 7. Cotton blouse and dress inspired by Russian folk traditions, S/S 06. 8. Design sketches, A/W 06.

3

‘The craziest ideas and unexpected materials can be adapted for everyday life’
Alena Akhmadullina

8

1

2

3

London-born Australian designer Alice McCall spent ten years as a successful stylist, working with such music icons as Kelis, Blondie, Marianne Faithfull and Natalie Imbruglia, as well as presenters on MTV London, before embarking on a career in fashion. In her spare time McCall had begun to make one-off silk tops and 1950s-style customized vintage dresses, marking the crossover from stylist to designer.

Alice McCall___8/100

After being headhunted by funky label Buddhist Punk to design their women's Spring/Summer 02 collection, McCall went on to work for Sass & Bide before launching her own label at Australian Fashion Week in 2004. In 2005, her 'Femininity Contrasted with Boldness' Spring/Summer collection won great praise from the buyers at Bloomingdale's: 'Alice McCall has that energy. She's on the same level as Marc by Marc Jacobs, Anna Sui and Jill Stuart.' The designer showed her 'Centre of Gravity' collection at London Fashion Week in 2006, and in the same year a line of party dresses designed by McCall for Target sold out in a week.

Combining elements of girlish charm and a bohemian flair, McCall's collections are always mixed up with a rock and roll attitude. 'I aim to create clothes that are desirable and stand the test of time,' she explains. 'To have a signature aesthetic that transcends fashion yet remains fashionable.'

McCall's success has been rapid, with her clothes now available in over ninety boutiques and department stores worldwide. Key to the success of the label is her unpretentious music-infused sensibility. She describes it as 'whimsical yet graphic, defined by pretty shapes brought to life with strong prints and precious detailing'. McCall enjoys the freedom that being creative offers. 'I was never one to obey rules. I love that it allows your creative instinct to come to life in a functional outlet.' To be contemporary is also paramount to McCall's vision. By pioneering the use of new fabrics and breathing life into old techniques, McCall communicates a modern reflection of the current zeitgeist in fashion.

www.alicemccall.com

1. 'Shooting Stars' t-shirt and black shorts, 'The Innocents', S/S 07. 2. Embroidered silk-chiffon blouse and silk-satin high-waist pencil skirt, 'The Voyant Lovers', S/S 08. 3. Peacock-print leggings and 'Electric eel' lock belt, 'Call of the Wild', A/W 07. 4. 'Toile de jour' print, S/S 08. 5. 'Vanilla Sandman' long coat, S/S 07. 6. 'Puff Adder' playsuit, A/W 07. 7. Cotton voile blouse and high-waist panel skirt in 'toile du jour' print, S/S 08. 8. Exposed zipper tights, 'Welcome to the Doll's House', Cruise 07. 9. 'Hidden Chameleon' military playsuit, A/W 07. 10. Crochet singlet with double-lock belt, A/W 07.

4

5

6

7

'I aim to create clothes that are desirable and *stand* the test of time'____Alice McCall

1

2

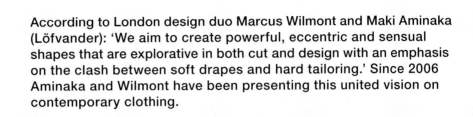

According to London design duo Marcus Wilmont and Maki Aminaka (Löfvander): 'We aim to create powerful, eccentric and sensual shapes that are explorative in both cut and design with an emphasis on the clash between soft drapes and hard tailoring.' Since 2006 Aminaka and Wilmont have been presenting this united vision on contemporary clothing.

Aminaka Wilmont___9/100

Wilmont studied menswear at Central Saint Martins and the Royal College of Art in London. Winning Collection of the Year at the International Talent Support (ITS#5) competition in Italy in 2006, he then worked as a freelance designer and consultant for several fashion labels and undertook fashion illustration for magazines. Aminaka graduated from University College of Borås in Sweden after studying womenswear. She moved to London and worked for designers Robert Cary-Williams, Clare Tough, Ann-Sofie Back and Sophia Malig. The pair met whilst working for Robert Cary-Williams.

'It is difficult to say exactly what inspires us as it is always a wide variety of themes, but generally our collections flirt curiously with and question the idea of shape and silhouette. A lot of our inspiration comes from eccentric and powerful real-life characters.' The designers strive to visualize the worlds inside their minds, attempting to bring these concepts into their clothes. 'Usually the design process unfolds from a story where we describe the characters and then make their clothes,' they explain. 'We research the inspiration that initiated the story and build on the technical aspects in terms of overall shape, silhouette and fabrics. As toileing begins and the characters come to life they start dictating the collection's direction and they can be quite pushy.'

Hand-printing and fabric manipulation emphasize the soft drapes and hard tailoring apparent in their clothes. Working mostly with traditional fabrics the team applies its skill to fine wool, elegant cotton and silks that are embellished with leather detailing to create a look of exclusivity and elegance. They describe their clients as fashion-conscious, high-end men or women.

www.aminakawilmont.com

1. Men's jacket, A/W 06. 2. Sleeveless dress with braces, S/S 07. 3. Textile print, A/W 07. 4. Longsleeved top with printed scarf, A/W 07. 5. Elasticated-waist miniskirt and blouse with bib detail, A/W 07. 6. Men's waistcoat and pants, A/W 06. 7–8. Low-back top and pants; v-neck tunic with printed polo neck. All A/W 07.

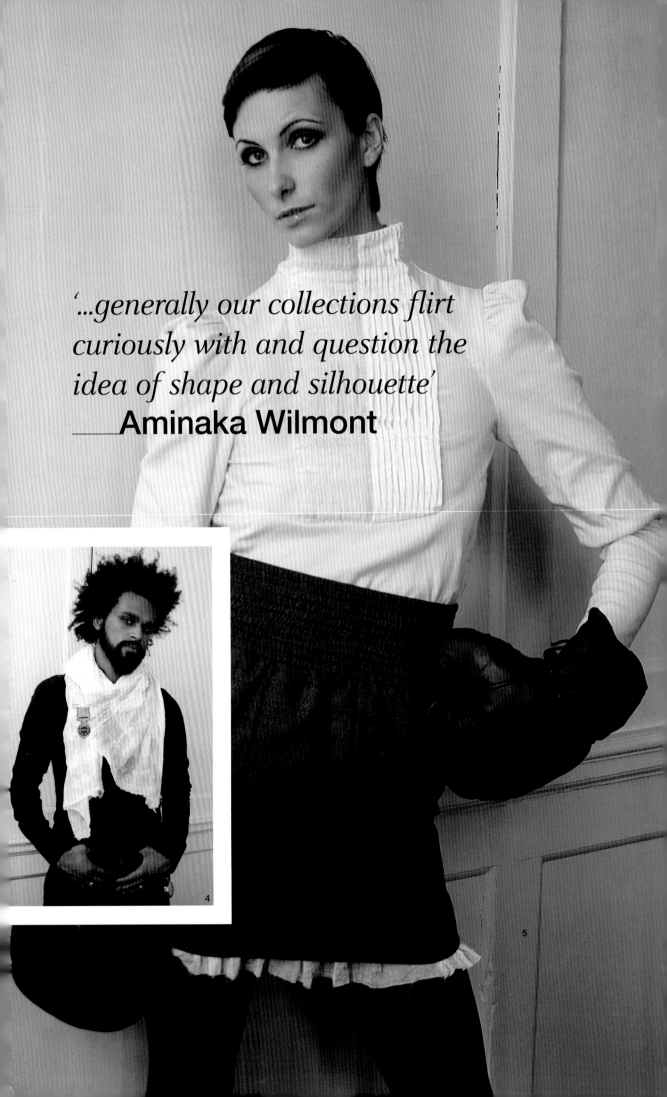

'...generally our collections flirt curiously with and question the idea of shape and silhouette'
___Aminaka Wilmont

6

7

8

1

2

Antoine Peters's design philosophy is based on 'wearing, watching and bringing a smile to' his customer. After studying at the Academy of Art and the Fashion Institute in Arnhem, Peters undertook work experience, first with Viktor & Rolf and then at the Dutch magazine *Avantgarde*. He was a finalist at the international Mittelmoda fashion awards in 2005 and 2006.

Antoine Peters___ *10/100*

When developing projects, his label and collaborations, Peters aims to raise his profile within the industry. His 'A Sweater For The World!' project is a two-person sweater that he would like to see as many people as possible photographed in. 'This big series of pictures is a weird, fun collection of people, showing one world with different kinds of styles, ages, points of view, values, religions and imagination. The "A Sweater For The World!" can also be worn by one person as an elegant evening gown. The sweater is sporty, elegant, sexy, playful, humorous, wearable and a spectacle at the same time. A graphic, colourful style in a world where nothing can be taken for granted,' explains Peters, who presented the photographs at Amsterdam's International Fashion Week in 2006.

Essentially practical and playful, Peters's designs are based on his interpretation of the classics – the t-shirt, jeans and sweater. Detailing, fabric and the exaggeration of proportion define his distinct look. 'In all my designs I capture this combination of humour, sex, ease-of-wear and elegance within the piece itself by pattern, detail or print design,' he says.

'Creating, telling, showing and giving a positive feeling' is key to Peters's design ideas, and he captures his concepts in little books, entitled *'Le petit Antoine'*, that he always carries around with him. The practical side of production, marketing and making the product and the label work in a commercial way is a main focus for Peters, as his vision is to achieve the ultimate: 'to design spectacular things without losing sight of the pragmatism within that same design'.

www.antoinepeters.com

1. Silk dress, S/S 07. 2. Printed silk-jersey dress showing images from the ongoing 'Sweater for the World' project. 3. T-shirt print, S/S 08. 4. Shiny denim jacket from the S/S 08 collection, which was based around classic items such as t-shirts, jeans and sweaters. 5. 'T-shirt' hat, S/S 08. 6. Photos from the 'Sweater for the World' project. 7. Cover for S/S 08 Lookbook.

'Creating, telling, showing and giving a positive feeling'
___Antoine Peters

4

5

1

Greek-born Apostolos Mitropoulos graduated from Veloudakis Fashion College in Greece in 1997. His career began by designing outfits for club dancers and theatrical performers. He opened his showroom in the centre of Athens in 2000 and presented his first fashion show in Paris at the Carousel du Louvre in February 2001. The following year he won the Madame Figaro Magazine Award for Best New Greek Designer. In 2006 Mitropoulos launched his own diffusion line in collaboration with Underground Fashion Company.

Apostolos Mitropoulos
_____11/100

Describing his aesthetic as kinky meets elegance, Mitropoulos states, 'I want to bring out the dynamic side in a woman and make her look powerful and sexy. I consider my clothes to be quite classic. I think that my lifestyle is what makes me modern.' His work is informed by sex and music, and Mitropoulos travels the world to find inspiration for his collections.

Collaborations for advertising campaigns comprise a key part of the designer's work. He has produced promotional designs for such companies as Coca-Cola, McDonalds, Vodafone, Lucky Strike and Absolut Vodka.

The most enjoyable part of design for Mitropoulos is the construction of the garment: taking a 2D pattern and turning it into a 3D item of clothing ready to be worn. Forming the pattern is challenging but he explains, 'the pattern is the architecture of clothing'. Not admitting to any prescribed creative process, Mitropoulos says he simply 'goes with the flow'. Contemporary fashion, for him, is concerned with 'recycling ideas of the past in new materials'.

Mitropoulos is a favourite in his homeland and he dresses celebrities, the high-fashion crowd and pop stars. He defines his customers in one word: 'rich'.

www.apostolosm.com

1. Silk-chiffon gown, A/W 08. 2. Wool and viscose dress with side split, A/W 07. 3. Super-jersey cut-away dress, A/W 05. 4. Black silk-jersey dress, S/S 07. 5-8. Super-jersey dress, wrap-top and leggings, A/W 06. 9. Loose blouson with tie-bottom leggings, A/W 08.

2

'I want to bring out the dynamic side in a woman and make her look powerful and sexy'
___Apostolos Mitropoulos

5

6

7

8

9

1

2

'Quirky, sexy, sophisticated, sporty and glamorous,' is how Ashish Gupta describes his contemporary designs. His clothes have received international recognition for their distinctive aesthetic that celebrates the best of Western and Eastern cultures.

Ashish____*12/100*

Born in Delhi, Ashish studied fine art in India before moving to the UK to undertake a degree in fashion design at Middlesex University. He went on to gain an MA from Central Saint Martins in 2000. After leaving college, Ashish began creating bespoke designs for friends and was spotted by Yeda Yun, the buyer for Browns Focus, who gave him his first order in 2001. In 2004 his vibrant and exuberant collection exploded on to the runway at London Fashion Week, winning him the New Generation Award for rising talent, which he also won in 2005 and 2006.

Ashish's collections are a dynamic mixture of slouchy sportswear and full-on glamour, infused with an obsession for detailed craftsmanship. 'Even a basic tee can be hand-sewn with a thousand glass beads to make it special,' explains Ashish, 'fabulous but casual'. The intricate handcrafted pieces are all manufactured in his own London studio and factory in India. Print is also used, as are woven and embroidered fabrics that balance sophistication with edginess: 'I love working with colour and light, hence my obsession with palettes and with developing new surface techniques.'

For Ashish, his customer is someone with a sense of humour, someone who likes to dress up but be dressed down at the same time. He believes contemporary fashion is constantly moving and hard to define, describing it as 'a reflection of an ever-changing social, cultural and political zeitgeist'. Inspired by an ever-changing global environment, Ashish's work is informed by diverse sources including 'friends, travelling, markets, films, music, books, people, life! It's hard to say what is going to be inspiring next, you just have to let it happen.'

www.ashish.co.uk

1–2. Multicoloured sequin tweed coat, A/W 07. **3.** Sequined coat with faux collar detail, A/W 07. **4.** Cerulean sequined dress, A/W 07. **5–6.** Wool corset dress; silver sequined bomber and skirt. A/W 06. **7.** White dress, S/S 08. **8.** Tarmac-print top and shorts, S/S 07.

3

5

4

6

8

'I love working with colour and light, hence my obsession with palettes and with developing new surface techniques'____Ashish

7

1

2

3

Popular definitions of glamour and beauty are challenged in Avsh Alom Gur's clothes. His designs combine Eastern and Western influences fused with urban street graffiti and grunge. After graduating with distinction from the MA fashion course at Central Saint Martins in London, Gur worked for Donna Karan as an eveningwear designer. He then went on to consult for Roberto Cavalli, Chloé and Nicole Farhi before starting his own label.

Avsh Alom Gur___*13/100*

In 2005 *Avsh Alom Gur* won the New Generation Award, sponsored by Topshop and the British Fashion Council, which allowed Gur to launch his Spring/Summer 06 collection at London Fashion Week. He received this award for outstanding new design talent three seasons in a row.

Underlying his design philosophy is the belief that 'the garment should work for you and not the other way around. My garments fit everyone. I create garments for women that treat their wardrobes as though they are curators of a gallery and want to express their own personalities'.

The designer draws inspiration from ethnic arts and crafts, in particular the distinctive Arabic dress of the Bedouin tribes. Making generous use of fabric to create space between the garment and the body, Gur often uses transparent printed and hand-dyed chiffons and delicate silks in harmony with rough tattered cottons. Some garments, like his lavish wrap-arounds, often incorporate exotic jewellery, such as hand-carved onyx. These contrasts of fabrics, textures and embellishments give his collections a sophisticated appeal with an unmistakable character.

An integral part of Gur's evolving design process is his collaborations with new artists whose talents span a range of disciplines, from jewellery-making and hand carving to knitting, knotting and print-making. Gur's work is informed by diverse sources, and he explains, 'Anything and everything from my daily vision inspires me. I can usually find something unique and beautiful in what others might think of as mess or dirt'.

www.avshalomgur.com

1. Moulded felt hat, S/S 05. **2.** Silk dresses, backstage at the A/W 06 show. **3.** Silk printed dress styled with cotton twisted belt and hand-carved birds made from semi-precious stones, S/S 06. Print by textile designer Daniel Reynolds for Avsh Alom Gur. **4.** Artwork by Daniel Reynolds, S/S 06.

1

2

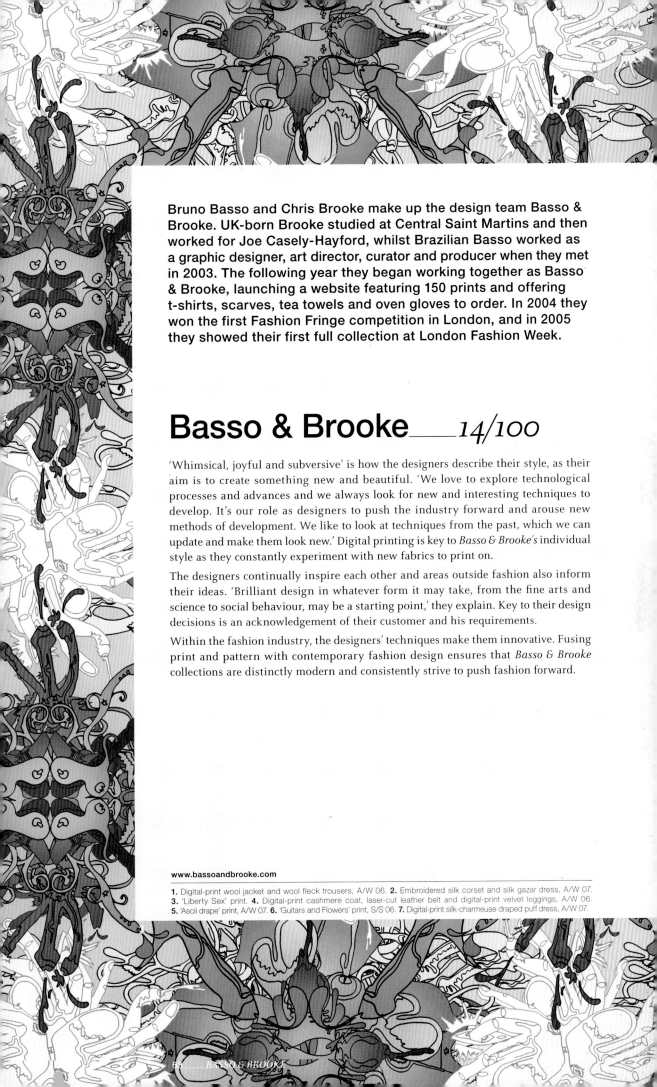

Bruno Basso and Chris Brooke make up the design team Basso & Brooke. UK-born Brooke studied at Central Saint Martins and then worked for Joe Casely-Hayford, whilst Brazilian Basso worked as a graphic designer, art director, curator and producer when they met in 2003. The following year they began working together as Basso & Brooke, launching a website featuring 150 prints and offering t-shirts, scarves, tea towels and oven gloves to order. In 2004 they won the first Fashion Fringe competition in London, and in 2005 they showed their first full collection at London Fashion Week.

Basso & Brooke___14/100

'Whimsical, joyful and subversive' is how the designers describe their style, as their aim is to create something new and beautiful. 'We love to explore technological processes and advances and we always look for new and interesting techniques to develop. It's our role as designers to push the industry forward and arouse new methods of development. We like to look at techniques from the past, which we can update and make them look new.' Digital printing is key to *Basso & Brooke's* individual style as they constantly experiment with new fabrics to print on.

The designers continually inspire each other and areas outside fashion also inform their ideas. 'Brilliant design in whatever form it may take, from the fine arts and science to social behaviour, may be a starting point,' they explain. Key to their design decisions is an acknowledgement of their customer and his requirements.

Within the fashion industry, the designers' techniques make them innovative. Fusing print and pattern with contemporary fashion design ensures that *Basso & Brooke* collections are distinctly modern and consistently strive to push fashion forward.

www.bassoandbrooke.com

1. Digital-print wool jacket and wool fleck trousers, A/W 06. **2.** Embroidered silk corset and silk gazar dress, A/W 07.
3. 'Liberty Sex' print. **4.** Digital-print cashmere coat, laser-cut leather belt and digital-print velvet leggings, A/W 06.
5. 'Ascii drape' print, A/W 07. **6.** 'Guitars and Flowers' print, S/S 06. **7.** Digital-print silk-charmeuse draped puff dress, A/W 07.

'Brilliant d...   ...whatever form
it may ta... f...   the fine arts
and scien...   ...cial behaviour,
may be a s... ...g point'
Basso ... Brooke

7

1

2

3

4

Danish Sarah Elbo is the designer behind Bo Van Melskens. Now Berlin-based, the line was formerly known as Sarah Heart Bo. Elbo's work has always been influenced and inspired by Bo, her imaginary friend and muse, and the collections reflect the designer's private stories. 'There is no philosophy,' explains Elbo, 'only a story to be continued'.

Bo Van Melskens___*15/100*

For Elbo, it was an intuitive decision to name her work after her muse. The fantasy friend Bo lives its life while Elbo makes sure to capture it in her work. 'You can actually read the collection if you are willing to. Bo enjoys its life with flawless ready-to-wear clothes,' says Elbo.

Describing her design style as elegance with an edge, Elbo produces quirky collections that aim to be cool and opinionated. Dresses and jersey pieces are signature garments, while colours and empty spaces are vital to the aesthetic. Elbo defines the look as, 'The imperfection of elegance ready to be inherited by the next generation'.

During the creative process, Elbo thrives. 'Having something in mind, making it happen, realizing that the item works and then seeing it being worn making this world a bit more exciting is fantastic.' Elbo believes that her talent lies in being able to pick up on a feeling or atmosphere that she is able to translate through her stories and ultimately her clothes. She does not draw but writes down the concept for her collections. 'I write the stories down on paper, but one month later I feel I have to make a better one,' she says. She blogs her ideas on her website, which in turn informs the next collection. Elbo's design process may be unconventional but her clothes are focused, sharp and inherently modern as she strives to 'keep reality away'.

www.bovanmelskens.com

1–4. Metallic slim dress with dark-flower print and underwear leggings; longsleeved underwear top and leggings with wide belt by Veil of Politeness; sunshine dress; dark-flower print metallic skirt and shortsleeved underwear top. All S/S 08. **5.** Underwear leggings, S/S 08.

5

1

2

Bora Aksu's clothes are characterized by complex cutting techniques that allow fabrics to move freely. His signature blend of silks, chiffons, tulles and distressed cotton t-shirts fused with underwear details and seams has brought Aksu international recognition.

Bora Aksu___*16/100*

Turkish-born Aksu graduated from Central Saint Martins in 2002, his collection attracting praise from the world's fashion press and also from Dolce & Gabbana, who purchased several pieces. In February 2003 Aksu made his debut during the off-schedule catwalk shows at London Fashion Week, where he received the Topshop New Generation Award for new design talent. The following season he was placed on the official London Fashion Week calendar.

Aksu's Spring/Summer 04 collection drew inspiration from such everyday objects as stripy bed covers, kitchen towels and old-fashioned undergarments that he reworked into feminine and contemporary shapes. The designs caught the attention of leading department stores including Liberty and Selfridges in the UK and Barneys in the USA.

'I believe fashion is more of a way of expressing someone's individuality rather than just a simple way of covering the body parts,' states Aksu. 'It is a unique language that has a visual voice. For me anything can drive fashion. It can be a movie, a piece that you found in a local car-boot sale, even a t-shirt that you've been wearing since you were 15.' Aksu predicts that fashion will never again become a statement as it was in the 1950s or 1960s because 'the world is changing so quickly, and women are more aware of what they like and who they are rather than following the mainstream fashion trends'.

Both research and experimentation are key to Aksu's creative process; he explains, 'I love researching as it opens doors to the places that I have never been before.' For Aksu, experimentation determines that his concepts can work in reality and also evolves his designs, as he believes 'you can have accidental results, which usually lead you into great design ideas. During the creative process too much planning does not allow any freedom and therefore you always need to leave a space to be free'.

www.boraaksu.com

1. Purple chiffon knit dress with sequins, S/S 07. 2. Hand knitted dress, A/W 07. 3. Illustrations by Bora Aksu. 4. Cream chiffon knit dress with metal embellishments, A/W 07. 5. Illustrations by Bora Aksu. 6. Garnet silk mini-dress with metal breast plate, made to order, A/W 07.

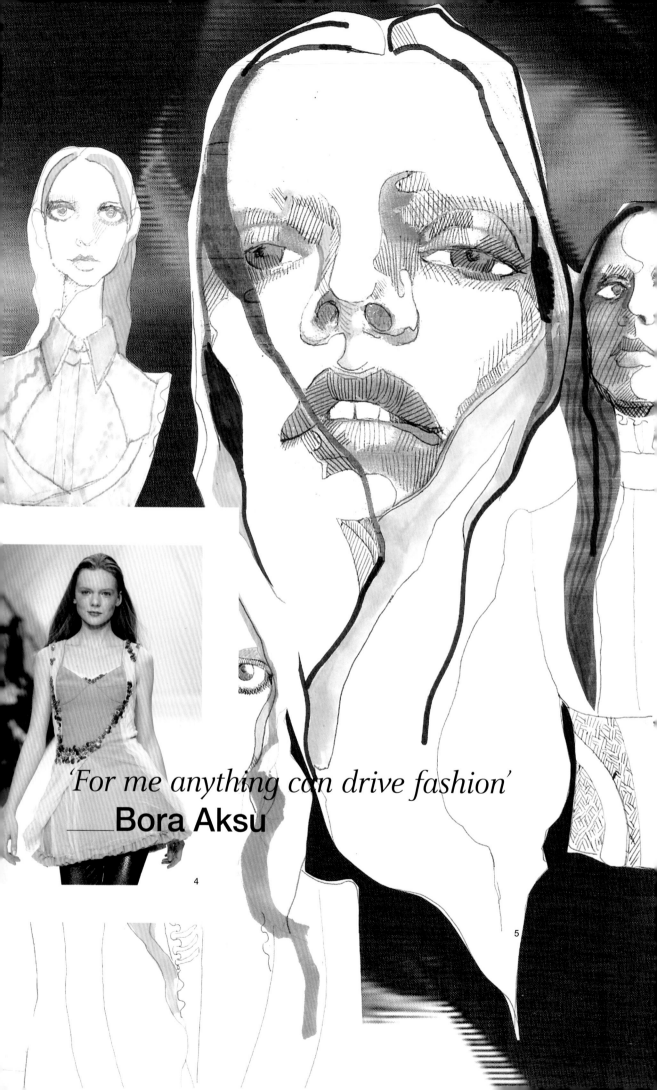

'For me anything can drive fashion'
Bora Aksu

4

5

6

1

2

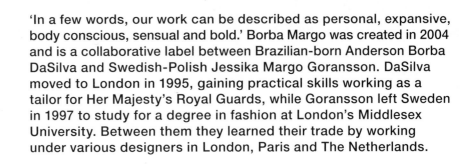

'In a few words, our work can be described as personal, expansive, body conscious, sensual and bold.' Borba Margo was created in 2004 and is a collaborative label between Brazilian-born Anderson Borba DaSilva and Swedish-Polish Jessika Margo Goransson. DaSilva moved to London in 1995, gaining practical skills working as a tailor for Her Majesty's Royal Guards, while Goransson left Sweden in 1997 to study for a degree in fashion at London's Middlesex University. Between them they learned their trade by working under various designers in London, Paris and The Netherlands.

Borba Margo___17/100

Borba Margo started out as a womenswear-focused label, but it gradually redirected towards accessories made from leather, metal and fabrics. 'We see our accessories as products with functional and decorative qualities,' they explain. 'Our collections are based on contrasts and how things are put together through unexpected combinations. We like to use familiar objects in an unfamiliar way. The way we work is similar to the process of clothing design as we use patterns and model on the stand.'

The design duo's work goes beyond the functional and decorative, with their use of cut and construction reflecting their fashion design background. 'We are one another's biggest source of inspiration and information. Working as a duo we have the advantage of a double measure of impressions. We completely share, trust and understand each other's enthusiasm, vision, thought and judgment,' they state.

Playing with illusions, *Borba Margo* is 'inspired by materials, their composition, possibilities and limitations'. DaSilva and Goransson create crossover designs, with accessories becoming jewellery and jewellery becoming accessories. Their process questions form, concept and context: 'The process is constant and fluid; ideas and research are always underway.' Before the team starts a collection they research an idea and then sit down and design together. 'It is not only about taking decisions together, it is about sparking each other's creativity and imagination. We aim to be genuine, to let our integrity, spirit and enthusiasm rule as our primary trademark and to constantly challenge ourselves.'

www.borbamargo.rendez-vous-paris.com

1. Bag with circular shoulder strap, A/W 07. **2.** Rosette belt in red suede folded in a ribbon, S/S 07. **3.** Orange and brown small circular bags, A/W 07. **4.** Floating Hula belt, S/S 07. **5.** Circular zip-on bumbag. Also functions as a handbag, with the belt used as a shoulder strap. A/W 07. **6.** Wide black leather belt with attached coin purse, S/S 07. **7.** Gloves with zip and detachable purse, A/W 07.

'We like to use *familiar* [...] an unfamiliar way'
___**Borba Margo**

4

5

6

7

Berlin-based Clara Leskovar and Doreen Schulz are the two designers behind c.neeon. They formed the label, the title being an amalgamation of their childhood nicknames, whilst studying at the School of Art and Design in Berlin. Graduating in 2004, they won the Galeries Lafayette fashion competition, which resulted in an exhibition at Galeries Lafayette in Paris. They also won the main fashion prize at the Hyères Festival International des Arts de la Mode in 2005. As a consequence, London Fashion Week invited them to apply for the New Generation Award, which they were given, allowing them to present their own show at London Fashion Week.

c.neeon___18/100

c.neeon's collections use strong graphic prints, some of which are inspired by Mondrian. Their silhouettes have intriguing volume and architectural, asymmetrical shapes. 'The prints are always related to the pattern but it is not the case that Clara hands over finished fabrics to Doreen, who makes clothes out of them. The depth of a skirt's folds is determined by the width of the block stripes, just as the size of a print depends on the way a dress falls,' they explain.

Their immediate environment inspires the designers. 'Since 2005 we have been in our own atelier in Lichtenberg, where we share an old Kindergarten with other people including photographers, painters, graphic designers and writers. We do not only share the house, we also do projects together.'

For the design team, contemporary fashion is concerned with the body and with a tendency towards a more body-conscious design aesthetic with shapes that extenuate the silhouette. 'We like to evolve with each collection and further develop our approach to design, strengthening our own style and signature,' they say. Not sticking with a defined look or customer, the team likes to experiment: 'We do not clearly think about the target customer, but we do what feels right for us and hopefully this is appreciated by others. We like to surprise ourselves with the pieces we develop, and therefore the collections can vary in style and feel so that it is quite possible that the customers will change along with them.'

www.cneeon.de

1. Jacket and trousers, 'Daydream Nation', A/W 04. 2. 'Kazaguruma' print. 3–4. Collection inspired by Art Deco artist Tamara de Lempicka, 'Sharing Secrets', A/W 07. 5. Origami-inspired dress, 'Local Foreigner', S/S 07. 6. Cotton coat and pants, A/W 04. 7. Geometric prints, A/W 07. 8. Graphic print, 'Way too Blue'.

4

'We like to evolve with each collection and further develop our approach to design, strengthening our own style and signature'
___**c.neeon**

5

6

7

1

2

3

German-born Carola Euler studied dressmaking and tailoring in her hometown of Gießen before moving to London in 1999 to study fashion at Central Saint Martins. In March 2005 she was awarded an MA, and had by this time already gained valuable experience working for such designers as Alexander McQueen, Alfred Dunhill, Jonathan Saunders, Raf Simons and Kim Jones.

Carola Euler___*19/100*

After graduation, Euler went to work as an assistant menswear designer at J. Lindeberg in Stockholm before returning to London in 1999, where she was offered one of three showcases as part of Fashion East MAN, an initiative in association with UK fashion chain Topman to promote new menswear designers. This allowed her to create 'Without a Ride', her Spring/Summer 07 collection that debuted in September 2006 during London Fashion Week.

Describe your design philosophy. *Making real clothes that men actually do want to wear by using a kind of naive approach to luxury dressing.*

How would you define your aesthetic? *In Stephen Doig's words, 'Boyish but sophisticated. Obvious yet discreet. Fresh yet formal. A new-money, white-trash interpretation of how to dress up.'*

What is the most enjoyable part of design? *Seeing it all coming together in the way I envisaged it, or even better, the moment backstage before the first model walks out on the runway.*

Who or what informs your work? *My favourite book is* In the American West, *by Richard Avedon. I always like the idea of what people are wearing in the American midwest because I've never been there. I picture it as a style of accidental nothingness. It's this supermarket-type clothing that just happens to have a certain cut or colour randomly combined with each other by the wearer that I find so interesting. Two or three pieces always make an outfit, basically. No fuss.*

What is the most challenging aspect of design? *Editing. I'm not a fan of embellishment so I have no problems with throwing things out. I'm not happy until everything that can be taken away is gone. But deciding on what needs to go can be difficult. If you get a small thing wrong it can unbalance the whole collection.*

www.carolaeuler.com

1. Aqua suit with shoes by Carola Eula for Buddhahood, 'Luxury', SS/08. 2. Double-breasted trench, t-shirt and chino shorts, 'Without a Ride', SS/08. 3. Double-belted trench, S/S 07. 4. White bib shirt, S/S 08. 5. Blue cut-out shirt and white jeans, S/S 08. 6. Black t-shirt worn with RayBan Wayfarers, S/S 07. 7–11. Bib shirt with suit trousers; aqua suit with black twin-strap vest; suit jacket with short-belt shorts; aqua suit trousers; cut-out pleat shirt. All S/S 08.

4

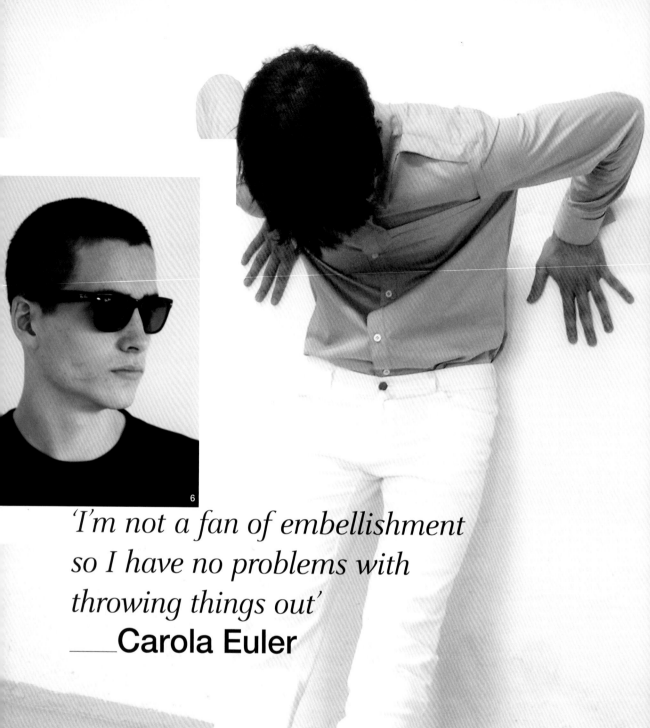

6

'I'm not a fan of embellishment so I have no problems with throwing things out'
___**Carola Euler**

7

8

9

10

11

83_____CAROLA EULER

Carri Mundane is the designer behind London-based label Cassette Playa. After studying fashion at Westminster University, Mundane launched her collection at a nightclub in London. It was immediately bought by the influential stores The Pineal Eye in London and Side by Side in Tokyo and she received acclaim for its edgy and colourful interpretation of contemporary fashion.

Cassette Playa___*20/100*

M.I.A., the British female rapper, and the Klaxons have both been dressed and had videos styled by Mundane. She is a contributing fashion editor of *Super Super* magazine, a stylist for *i-D* magazine and she has collaborated with Nicola Formichetti for *Dazed & Confused* magazine.

Mundane's collections are inspired by popular culture, from comic books to old-school technology. The label strives to push viewers' senses into overload, referencing drug culture, raves and the psychedelic, and attempting to recreate the associated experiences without any consumption.

Cassette Playa's clothes are what Mundane describes as 'mixed wear', essentially menswear that girls can also wear. Colour and prints are central themes, and the resulting garments include oversized velour tracksuit tops, tie-dye t-shirts, baggy tops with baggy shorts and blouson jackets all fused with kaleidoscopic prints in clashing neon tones. Mundane also reworks African prints and references kitsch 1980s cartoons.

Describe your design philosophy. *Cartoon couture. A luxury sport and streetwear brand.*

How would you define your aesthetic? *Graphic. Acieed. Future.*

What is the most enjoyable part of design? *I love researching, building a world. But the best bit has got to be the end when you actually have a product. The full stop is something real.*

How would you describe your customer? *Pixel warriors and future-thinking strong men battling real and virtual worlds.*

How would you describe your creative process? *24/7.*

Who or what informs your work? *Technology, music, comics, computer games, rituals and tribes.*

What is the most challenging aspect of design? *A designer isn't an artist. It can't be about my ego. It's always about a person and a product. I like these limits.*

www.cassetteplaya.com

1. Linking the real and virtual worlds, video still featuring Peaceman t-shirt, A/W 07. **2.** Dotty-face t-shirt and pants on the catwalk at MAN, S/S 07. **3–4.** Hallucinogenic acid brights, cartoon prints and oversized shapes combine to create sensory overload, S/S 07.

4

1

2

Graduating from La Cambre School of Visual Arts in her native Belgium, Cathy Pill went on to serve internships at A. F. Vandevorst and Vivienne Westwood. In 2003 she won Collection of the Year at Trieste's second International Talent Support contest (ITS#2). In 2005 she won sponsorships from La Fondation Pierre Bergé et Yves Saint Laurent and from La Maison Yves Saint Laurent at the ANDAM (Association Nationale pour le Développement des Arts de la Mode) contest in France. In the same year she was given the Fabio Inghirami Award in Italy and scooped the Modo Bruxellae Prize in Belgium.

Cathy Pill___*21/100*

Pill launched her first ready-to-wear collection during Paris Fashion Week in October 2005. Her Spring/Summer 06 collection, entitled 'Blink', was informed by Art Nouveau patterns and featured draped and bunched silhouettes. The collection was presented at Les Arts Décoratifs and immediately attracted the attention of the international press.

Creating modern and feminine silhouettes, Pill has become known for her innovative use of prints and shapes. 'I'm trying to transmit a feeling through shape, always searching for the right line in relation to the right print and/or fabric, so that the women who see or wear a piece of my clothing feel something unique,' she explains. 'I especially love the idea that everything has a sense of being, and every form is related within the global structure. I'm trying to create my clothes and collections with this thought.'

Defined by clear lines and strong relationships between colour and fabric, Pill's clothes are inspired by the Art Nouveau architecture and design of her homeland. She enjoys all aspects of the creative process, but particularly the beginning and the end: 'The moment when the first ideas are flashing in, the choosing of colours, prints, fabrics and shapes, a new chapter of a long story begins,' enthuses the designer. 'And then there is the end – the last details, the last-minute changes, when everything is coming together and you see your imagination taking life, when it begins to exist by itself, when you decide to close the chapter.'

www.cathypill.com

1. Asymmetric draped cocktail dress with graphic print, S/S 07. 2. Floral-print dress, S/S 06. 3. Crackle-effect printed textile, S/S 06. 4. Streamlined silhouette with bold print, A/W 06. 5. Catwalk show, A/W 06. 6. Silk slip dress with trompe l'oeil-effect printed necklace, S/S 07. 7. Geometric print with strong, geometrical silhouette, S/S 06. 8. Graphic-print scarf, A/W 07.

'I especially love the idea that everything has a sense of being, and every form is related within the **global structure'__Cathy Pill**

4

5

6

7

8

Finnish Cecilia Sörensen studied tailoring in Helsinki before obtaining a degree in fashion design in 2001 in Barcelona, where she is now based. She worked for Antonio Miro before launching her own collection in 2002, the same year in which she won Young Designer of the Year at ModaFAD. Sörensen has two stores in Barcelona: a designer's collective called Comité, which opened in 2002, and she is also co-owner of Bingo Shop, established in 2006. She has shown her collections several times at Circuit and Barcelona Fashion Week.

Cecilia Sörensen___*22/100*

Sörensen describes her style as 'clean, sensitive, romantic and pure'. Her garments fuse contrasts between the feminine and the masculine, and her Scandinavian functionalism is juxtaposed with her surroundings in Barcelona. Informed by eclectic influences, she explains, 'My life, my rooms that I have, my things, my books, my dreams, my memories, my family photographs, old photos found in the street, early documentary photography (like August Sander), exhibitions, books, dressmaking and tailoring are all inspirational'.

The designer's creative process involves researching, drawing and then sampling. 'Building up my own small micro-cosmos of my vision with certain colours, fabrics, shapes and details. I work with sketchbooks, modelling on a dummy and then classic pattern cutting.' Sörensen designs two womenswear collections: 'Cecilia Sörensen' and 'Pequeños Héroes'. The latter uses recycled materials and fabrics including antique sheets, pillowcases, men's shirts and waistcoats. Dresses and skirts, for example, are cut out from sheets one by one, emphasizing the original handmade embroideries and lace trimmings, before being dyed in the colours of the collection. Men's shirts are transformed into women's sizes by pleats and gathering, while men's tailored waistcoats are turned into bags.

Creating unique pieces with a strong ecological stance and working with recycled material, Sörensen produces her entire collection in a small dressmaker's workshop in Barcelona. Producing collections locally and in an ethically correct manner is, Sörensen believes, the luxury of the future.

www.ceciliasorensen.com

1. Round-collared jacket, A/W 07. 2. Flower-embroidered viscose blouse, S/S 08. 3. Pleated polkadot dress, S/S 07. 4. Fabric, A/W 02. 5. Cotton trench, A/W 06. 6. Gathered t-shirt, S/S 08. 7–8. Navy summer dress; cotton tie-front blouse and skirt, S/S 07. 9–10. Garment details, A/W 02.

4

'Clean, sensitive, romantic and pure' **Cecilia Sörensen**

7

8

9

10

1

2

In 2003 Chris Liu set up his womenswear label after graduating with distinction from the MA course in fashion design at the London College of Fashion. Born in Urumqi in northwest China, Liu had access from an early age to Western art and fashion magazines, and his childhood was informed by an awareness of multiculturalism. This juxtaposition of creative freedom set against the bold symbolism of Chinese propaganda acted as a powerful catalyst for his creative inspirations.

Chris Liu___*23/100*

Liu moved to New Zealand in 2003 to work for knitwear label Sabatini for four years. This was followed by a period in Hong Kong working for a high-street brand, where he developed and established a seasonal collection. It was here that Liu learned the potential of the Chinese market and discovered how the Hong Kong fashion industry was able to successfully adapt to the domestic markets of its neighbours.

Combining creativity and commercialism, Liu creates quality high-style clothing that appeals to an international market: 'The collection is not country-specific,' he says, 'it is designed for professional women worldwide. It is about setting a standard, highlighting the international aspects and mixed identity of the brand and reflecting beautiful, confident, sexy women.'

The designer's aesthetic is concerned with practicality, and being commercially aware gives him a focus. Described as a 'luxury brand in the making', the line appeals to stylish and self-aware women who know what they like. Liu is inspired by classical music, literature, myths and folk legends, old movies and photography, and insists that he enjoys all aspects of the design process, 'from primary research to the final stage line-up with the stylist. The most enjoyable thing for me is working with a group of talented and creative people'.

www.chrisliulondon.com

1. Silk jacket with leather trim detail, S/S 06. **2.** Silk wrap-coat with leather trim, A/W 05. **3.** Shoulder-padded viscose dress, A/W 07. **4.** Silk dress with Swarovski crystals, A/W 06. **5–8.** Wool coat; heavy-wash denim dress; bow-detail silk dress; velvet top with quilted skirt. All A/W 07. **9.** Layered silk dress with zip detail, A/W 06. **10.** Belted wool sweater.

3

9

10

'The collection is not country-specific, it is designed for professional women worldwide'
___**Chris Liu**

1

2

3

During his time at the Royal Academy of Fine Arts in Antwerp, German Christoph Fröhlich undertook work experience at Dries Van Noten and Tim Van Steenbergen. He graduated in 2005 and was given an award by the Flemish government to encourage innovation and creativity. In the same year he won the Diesel award at the International Talent Support Competition (ITS#4) in Trieste, Italy. Following this he designed a mini-collection of five garments that were produced by Diesel and distributed in twelve Diesel stores worldwide, complete with a personalized label bearing his name. In 2006 Fröhlich won the Becks Fashion Award for innovation in German fashion design. The award gave him the opportunity to showcase his work at a professional catwalk show at the Bread & Butter trade show in Barcelona.

Christoph Fröhlich___24/100

'My work is a never-ending process,' states Fröhlich. 'It's an observation on daily life, a reflection of experiences. My aim is to stay constantly curious.' Intent on finding new ways to morph garments, details and styles, Fröhlich employs an experimental deconstructivist approach to his design process, which could be described as deconstruction in order to reconstruct. 'I try to redefine shapes, patterns, lines, tailoring and craftsmanship to add another dimension.' He finds inspiration in ideas, his friends, research and in the actual process of making clothes. 'The creative journey forms an idea and the steps to build up something new from it. This is an endless evolution that reflects the present, but almost every time is actually referring to the past,' he explains.

Fröhlich believes that his customers are urban and young with an appreciation of craftsmanship and an eye for detail. His innovation in design reflects his own experiences: 'My work is attached to my everyday life. I try to personally reflect what I see, think and feel in the moment. Therefore I guess a certain zeitgeist is reflected without trying hard to be too innovative.'

www.christophfroehlich.de

1. Graduate collection show in Barcelona, A/W 06. 2–4. Patchwork cape with silicone print hoody; overprinted parka; cotton blazer with zip chains. All A/W 06. 5. Hooded sweatshirt, S/S 07. 6–9. Cool-wool blazer; c-cut leather pants and cotton-wool parka; c-cut leather pants and double-layered cool-wool blazer; reconstructed trench. All graduate collection, A/W 06. 10. Engineered double-layered hoody, S/S 07.

6

7

5

8

9

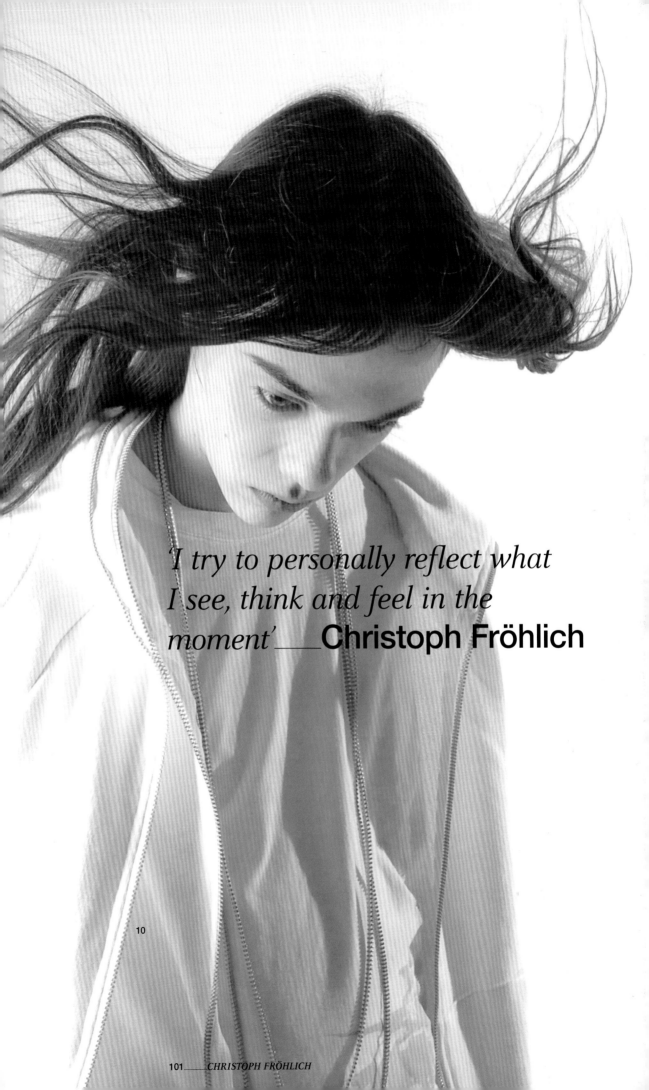

*'I try to personally reflect what I see, think and feel in the moment'*___**Christoph Fröhlich**

10

1

2

3

Japanese designers Kaito Hori and Iku Furudate established Commuun in 2005. Hori studied at New York's Fashion Institute and the Arnhem Academy of Art in The Netherlands before moving to Paris to work as an assistant at Balenciaga. Furudate trained at Tokyo's Bunka Fashion College and London's Central Saint Martins before she too moved to Paris to work with Anne Valérie Hash. After meeting in the French capital, Hori and Furudate decided to collaborate, employing a design philosophy that embraced 'a minimalist approach to structure, using natural fabrics to achieve something classical but new and functional'.

Commuun___25/100

When considering the future of fashion, the designers believe that environmental issues cannot be ignored, and hence favour Japanese organic cotton and Italian linen over chemical-based fabrics. Each collection is inspired by the natural landscape and the harmony and tensions found within nature. While the clothes are ecologically sound they also present a strong modern aesthetic through colour and cut. *Commuun* is spearheading the movement for sustainable clothing that simultaneously communicates design modernity.

The designers describe their aesthetic as being about 'carefully chosen fabrics with minimal and refined details'. Their design process begins with research into fabrics, deciding upon the right volume and cut before adding the fine details that give the garments their special characteristics: 'We like the process of looking at a fabric and trying to think of the best shape for it, and vice versa, finding the best fabric to suit the shape we have.' Hori and Furudate strive to find a timeless combination of fabric and cut in an attempt to create a new future classic, insisting 'We don't try to be innovative or modern, we just continue to do what we believe in.'

The clothes are intended for strong, independent women: 'We like to think of our customers as people who know how to choose for themselves,' explains the duo. 'Contemporary fashion, to us, is something that is made not only by designers but also with input from the end users.'

www.commuun.com

1. Vaporous white chiffon dress, S/S 07. 2–4. Wool-silk mix coat with pants; neon-yellow silk shirt with wool and silk skirt; neon-yellow pants. All A/W 07.

4

1

German Sabine Bräuninger graduated from the MA womenswear course at Central Saint Martins in 2001. After gaining industry experience with Hussein Chalayan and Robert Cary-Williams, Bräuninger decided to launch her own distinctive vision through Customers Own Property. The label was awarded New Generation sponsorship by the British Fashion Council, allowing Bräuninger to exhibit her collections during London Fashion Week and reach an international audience.

Customers Own Property
_____26/100

Bräuninger defines her philosophy as 'avoiding perfection. Fragments that don't entirely match (maybe by accident) within a calculated and organized framework make my designs more interesting and less predictable'. Her work embraces the 'ugly', or what is considered as ugly or unfashionable is recycled and introduced in a more modern design context. Bräuninger also cares about the wearer, believing that her garments should allow customers to participate in the design through styling and combining the garments with their own wardrobe.

The label supports the German artistic vision of intelligent, utilitarian and bold clothing. Bräuninger describes the line as 'understated, monochrome, user-friendly, unconventional and about proportion'. The collections, which offer both menswear and womenswear, are unique in that an emphasis is placed on the creative design process. Incorporating tailoring techniques with random details inspired by the everyday, the clothes often communicate the narrative of their creation. Signature elements are pieces of workwear and military-inspired clothing that often reference masculine tailoring and print.

For Bräuninger the research phase of her creative process and the development of a concept throughout the collection is a very enjoyable part of her work. 'Through stretching, scaling and the collage of picture fragments, new shapes and details can be found. This technique is then translated into patterns and simulated on the dressmaking dummy.' Bräuninger considers her customers to be informed about fashion designers and to be people who make a deliberate choice to buy *Customers Own Property*, maybe because the design philosophy interests them.

www.customersownproperty.com

1. Short trench cape, sleeveless hoody and slim-cut pinstripe suit, A/W 06. **2.** Design for show invitation, A/W 07. **3.** Plug necklace, S/S 05. **4.** Cotton shirt, inverted-pleat skirt and cummerbund with logo sequins, A/W 07. **5.** Short trench cape, circle-cut leather dress and hand printed tights, A/W 06. **6.** Design sketches, A/W 05. **7.** Digital-print dress with chandelier motif, A/W 05.

2

'Understated, monochrome, user-friendly, unconventional and about proportion'
___Customers Own Property

5

6 ②

7

2

3

4

5

Whilst at Central Saint Martins, Danielle Scutt was awarded the Chloe Award for best designer and also picked up the Lancôme Award for Modern Femininity. She graduated in 2005 and her debut at London Fashion Week the following year communicated her powerful and provocative portrayal of women in fashion.

Danielle Scutt___27/100

Inspired by the female characteristics of power and sexuality, Scutt's collections are dynamic and slick. She has quickly developed a niche look with her signature pieces, which include canvas fitted jackets and coats with puff sleeves and oversized pussybows that cover the shoulder line, pleated pencil skirts, high-waisted narrow trousers, spray-on catsuits and skin-tight silk-jersey leotards, singlets and vests. Oversized prints, matching hosiery and shoes, and wide belts that dictate super-skinny silhouettes have come to define the Scutt aesthetic.

Scutt describes her look as 'clothes you can have a fight in'. Referencing 1980s power dressing the clothes are provocative and distinctive. Using precise cutting skills, Scutt communicates a powerful attitude that is ultra glamorous but with a hint of rock and roll attitude. Her collections are strictly tailored and present an assertive and thoroughly modern silhouette.

How would you define your aesthetic? *Creating image and persona, enhancing the wearer.*

What is the most enjoyable part of design? *Research.*

How would you describe your customer? *Deluded.*

How would you describe your creative process? *Research, designing, drawing, toileing, sampling.*

How would you define contemporary fashion? *Fashion for now.*

Who or what informs your work? *A variety of things: people, personalities, animals and music.*

What is the most challenging aspect of design? *Technicalities.*

www.daniellescutt.com

1. Silk-jersey dress, dog-hair print, A/W 07. **2.** Pink wool and lamé skirt and lamé shirt, A/W 07. **3.** Screen-printed dress and gold and silver multiple chain, A/W 07. **4.** Black lingerie and marioboselli jersey dress, A/W 07. **5.** Pink wool skirt suit with lamé shirt, A/W 07. **6.** Mohair dress with gold and silver multiple chain, A/W 07.

1

2

3

Created in 2001, Denis Simachëv's label is a luxury Russian prêt-à-porter brand. The upside-down logo expresses the position of the label: 'We look at things from a different point of view. We find fashion has doubtful values and we like to laugh at ourselves and we don't take clothes too seriously.' Intentionally provocative, this viewpoint is key to the brand's aesthetic, which is concerned with making Russian design of European quality.

Denis Simachëv___*28/100*

Based on Russian history, culture and folk art, the label incorporates Russian traditions alongside contemporary fashion. Simachëv's approach to research is the central theme of every collection and usually references the folk ornaments, pattern and original crafts of Russia. 'My aim is to be precisely Russian. So many brands and designers now look the same, you can't tell the country of their origin. The Russian culture and history have so many ideas I can use, so many things that inspire me that I see my mission is to develop Russian fashion.'

Working with respected Western stylists and owning his own production facilities in Russia and Italy, Simachëv has the flexibility to create high-quality clothing and accessories in modern fabrics and materials. 'I can be inspired by anything I see – an old dress, furniture, the look of homeless people near my studio and so on. I have been inspired by gypsies for one collection and crime in 1990s Russia informed another collection.'

In Moscow, Simachëv's store and 24-hour bar is situated near other luxury brands such as Burberry, Dior and Louis Vuitton, but as Simachëv explains his customers are very different. 'It's an island of freedom surrounded by pompous boutiques. The concept is a shop on the first floor and a bar on the ground floor and each night the best DJs play music and people have fun. The atmosphere is very free and easy. The customers are people of different ages who don't take fashion seriously. They want to look different, are both proud to be Russian and have a sense of humour and irony with regard to themselves and also to their country's history.'

www.denissimachev.com

1. Gold-painted denim trousers and top, S/S 07. 2–3. Sheepskin-pile earflap cap and sheepskin cossack hat, A/W 05. 4. Traditional Russian GZHEL pattern from A/W 05 campaign. 5. Fur-pile cap and leather jacket, 'Chukotka', A/W 06. 6. Classic jacket and leggings, 'Gypsies', S/S 08. 7–8. Flagship store in Moscow. 9. Model wall for catwalk collection.

5

6

*'My aim is to be precisely Russian'*___Denis Simachëv

1

2

3

Scottish-born Deryck Walker studied fashion and textiles at Glasgow School of Art before moving to London, where he worked for Boudicca and Robert Cary-Williams. He then spent time in Milan working at Versace before returning to London and launching his debut menswear collection in 2005, which was sold in the prestigious Dover Street Market. In 2008 Walker introduced his first womenswear collection, a decision that evolved due to a growing customer-base of women who were wearing his men's garments.

Deryck Walker____29/100

Describe your design philosophy. *Everything I do is a small adjustment of something that already exists.*

How would you define your aesthetic? *I always start with a great classic or style. You can't go wrong if you work with a great foundation of the basics.*

How would you describe your customer? *Anybody who is into what I do; you should only wear clothes if you really like them. There's nothing worse than a forced look.*

How would you describe your creative process? *It depends: sometimes I go straight into the toile, or sometimes I start with a drawing or a point of inspiration.*

How would you define contemporary fashion? *It's hard to define with so many designers doing their own thing. I think you could define the 1940s and 1950s but now I'm not sure.*

Who or what informs your work? *Francis Bacon and James Dean. People who make a contribution to this world.*

What is the most challenging aspect of design? *Starting a new project.*

How are you personally innovative in fashion design? *By keeping myself out there with my eyes and ears open, keeping myself current.*

www.deryckwalker.com

1–2. Cape and slim trousers, 'Wizard', A/W 05. 3. Shirt and trousers with neon belt, 'Wizard vs Machine', A/W 06. 4. Shirt and trousers, 'Machine', S/S 06. 5. Self structure, 2006. 6. Shortsleeved shirt and long shorts, S/S 06. 7–10. Windmill mask; rounded kilt; tailored puffa jacket; long waistcoat. All 'Couture Boy', A/W 07.

4

'Everything I do is a small adjustment of something that already exists'___**Deryck Walker**

5

6

1

2

New York-based menswear label Duckie Brown is designed by Steven Cox and Daniel Silver. Cox is a former designer at Tommy Hilfiger and Silver previously worked as a daytime TV producer. In 2006 they were nominated for the Council of Fashion Designers of America (CFDA) Perry Ellis Award for Menswear, and they have exhibited their garments at the Victoria & Albert Museum in London.

Duckie Brown___*30/100*

Describe your design philosophy. *We start with the shoulder and work out. The cornerstone of every collection is the tailored jacket and tailored coat. From there everything comes naturally.*

How would you define your aesthetic? *SC: 23 years of living in the UK and 16 years of living in NYC, that kind of mix. DS: It's mine – comes from me – it's elegant and dishevelled. Think schoolboy in uniform with a wonky tie.*

What is the most enjoyable part of design? *We love every aspect of design from the thought process and sketching to the finished product. We embrace it all.*

How would you describe your customer? *We've been really delighted to discover that any man from age 20 to 83 is our customer. They all find something that suits them and we love that. We offer something for everyone.*

How would you describe your creative process? *Every collection is based on the lives we lead and where we travel. We are inspired by the world we live in – everything that surrounds us; everything that happens to us is reflected in our collection.*

How important is masculinity in menswear? *We think masculinity depends on the man wearing the clothing. How does he define himself? What is masculine?*

What is the most challenging aspect of design? *The business of the fashion business is the most difficult aspect of being a designer.*

www.duckiebrown.com

1. Giant-rose-print shirt and silk gazar trousers, S/S 08. 2. Corduroy jacket with low-crotch trousers and polo with beaded chandelier motif, A/W 04. 3. Turquoise fox chenille scarf and cap with feathers, A/W 04. 4. Silver python tote, S/S 08. 5. Corduroy suit with striped shirt, A/W 02. 6. Silver cotton shirts with Prince of Wales cotton trousers and cashmere beaded hats, S/S 07. 7. Sketches for the S/S 07 collection.

3

4

5

*'We are inspired by the world we live in – everything that surrounds us; everything that happens to us is reflected in our collection'*___**Duckie Brown**

6

7

1

2

Anna Figuera Delgado and Macarena Ramos Buil formed the label El Delgado Buil in 2004 and show their collections at Barcelona Fashion Week. In 2005 they presented 'Crazy Kids', their Autumn/Winter 05/06 collection, and 'Las Vegas', their Spring/Summer 06 line. In partnership with Flora and Lawhite, they set up their shop, Cuatroseis, in 2006 in Barcelona, where they have their studio and showroom. The collection for Autumn/Winter 07/08, 'My family goes to Oklahoma', won the L'Oréal prize for the best collection by new designers.

El Delgado Buil___*31/100*

'We are looking for the point between commerciality and creativity,' explain the designers, whose work communicates a youthful and fresh aesthetic. The customers they attract are both men and women. 'It is not about a specific age. It's just about feeling young,' they say.

Interested in exploring contrasts in their collections, the designers juxtapose big with small, natural materials with synthetics and modern shapes with classical forms. Their design process follows the same route each time: 'First we think about the collection theme and then we begin to search and investigate it. Then we look for the fabrics and we make the sketches. Finally we create the image and styling for the show.'

Inspiration is diverse: 'John Waters, Diane Arbus, Ramones, Terry Richardson, grandmothers, the United States, our friends, magazines, books like *Please Kill Me,* Sofia Loren and cowboys have all informed collections.' According to *El Delgado Buil,* it is a challenge to create things that people are going to enjoy, but their biggest reward is 'when the collection is finished and you feel like you have done good work'. The design team's collections have been well received by the international fashion press and the label is central to the establishment of Spain as an influential fashion capital.

www.eldelgadobuil.com

1. 'Crazy Kids' collection on the catwalk, A/W 05. 2. Mohair jersey featuring the face of designer Macarena's grandmother, 'My Family Goes to Oklahoma', A/W 07. 3. Striped shirt and jacket, 'Las Vegas', S/S 07. 4. Backstage at the S/S 07 show. 5. 'Divine' print t-shirt and organic silk trench, 'Dreamland', S/S 08 collection inspired by John Waters. 6. The designers wearing their 'Divine' print t-shirts with fringed leather scarves. 7. Pink leather baseball jacket and Liberty-inspired print shirt, A/W 05. 8. Illustration for sunglasses contest.

3

'We are looking for the point between commerciality and creativity'___**El Delgado Buil**

4

5

6

7

8

1

Emilio de la Morena was born in Alicante, Spain, where he studied sculpture. Moving to Britain in 1993, he gained a first class honours degree in business and commerce and joined a brand consultancy in London, working on very diverse projects. It was during this period that he developed an interest in fashion and consequently enrolled on a short course at Central Saint Martins. His portfolio gained him a place in the final year of the menswear degree at the college.

Emilio de la Morena____*32/100*

After graduating, de la Morena worked with Rafael Lopez and Jonathan Saunders before setting up his own label in 2006. He exhibited his first full collection at London Fashion Week in 2007, showing his first catwalk collection in a salon-style presentation, which received positive reviews from the press. His country is a key influence on his work and the inspiration for his Autumn/Winter 07/08 collection combined the Spanish tradition of bullfighting with intricate sculptural shapes.

Celebrating the female form, de la Morena's work mixes contemporary cuts with traditional Spanish influences. Inspiration comes from a wide range of sources, from sculpture to architecture, from ancient embroidery techniques to the native fashions of his homeland. 'We are a luxury womenswear label,' explains de la Morena, 'which teams highly creative work with an extraordinary level of quality and sophistication. The collections tend to be inspired by traditional Spanish techniques and craftsmanship making them really modern and fresh.'

When designing, de la Morena thrives on the research process and experimenting on the stand. 'The experience of creating new shapes and silhouettes whilst using inspiration from a wide scope of my own interests and developing them into something unique is enjoyable. The challenge is to create new ideas for each season and work with different techniques, and also to sustain an ongoing theme.'

According to the designer, his customers are powerful, sophisticated and self-confident women who have a sense of style and an awareness of fashion. 'A woman who has taken charge of her own life,' he states.

www.emiliodelamorena.com

1. Green wool bodice with silk-organza skirt, A/W 07. 2. Cashmere jacket with eyelets and red matador shirt and snood, A/W 07. 3. Illustrations by Kinga Malisz, A/W 07. 4. Short silk dress with cross-over strap detail, S/S 07. 5. Matador dress in jersey and silk tulle with leather and metal ornamentation, A/W 07. 6. Cotton shirt with ornamented bustier and leather skirt with cotton underskirt, A/W 07.

2

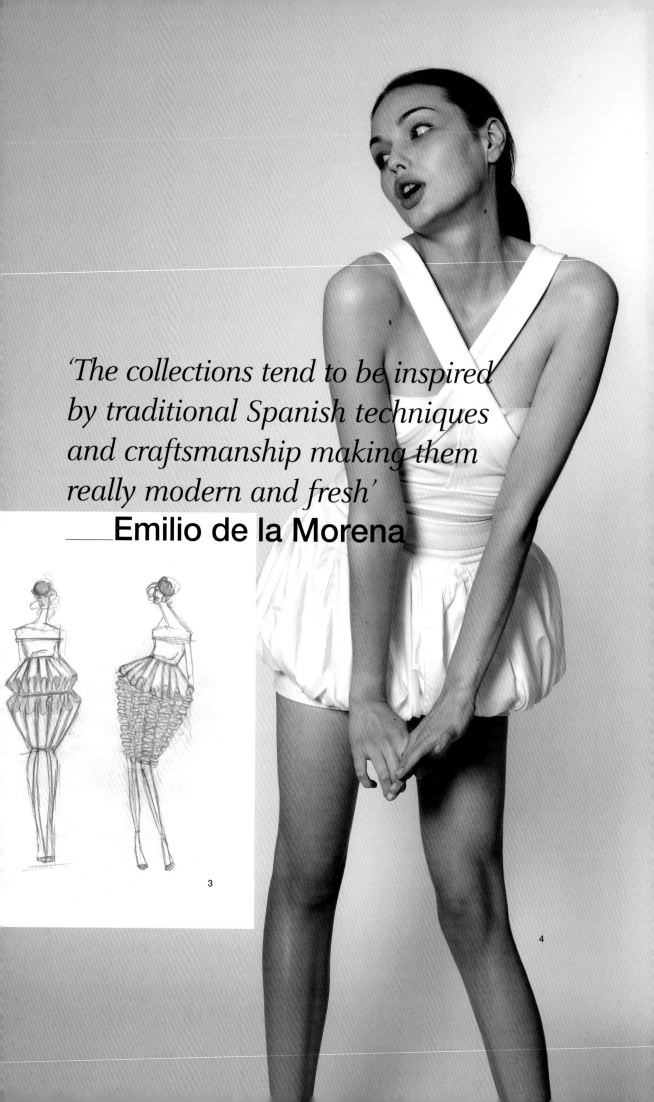

'The collections tend to be inspired by traditional Spanish techniques and craftsmanship making them really modern and fresh'
Emilio de la Morena

3

4

5

6

2

3

1

4

5

Starting out as a Classics student, Erdem Moralioglu went on to study fashion design at Ryerson University in Toronto, from where he moved to the UK to take up an internship at Vivienne Westwood. In 2000 he enrolled on the MA course in fashion at the Royal College of Art, focusing on print and textiles, and his widely acclaimed graduate collection closed the RCA Show in 2003.

Erdem___*33/100*

After graduation, Moralioglu worked as a design assistant for Diane von Furstenberg in New York before returning to London to launch his own line, *Erdem*, in 2005. The now UK-based designer won the Fashion Fringe Award in 2005 and debuted his collection during London Fashion Week.

The label fuses sharp tailoring with romanticism and bold and graphic custom-designed silk prints. Moralioglu delights in contrasts, whether a mix of masculine and feminine, print and plain, or dark with light, and he presents his vision with confidence.

Describe your design philosophy. *My work is always about contrast. The heavy mixed with the light, the feminine mixed with the masculine, the architectural mixed with organic free forms.*

How would you define your aesthetic? *My aesthetic is conservative mixed with something much darker. There is always a flip side to everything that I like; if I think something is beautiful there has to be one aspect of it slightly wrong for me to love.*

What is the most enjoyable part of design? *Research – throwing myself into a subject and then seeing it transform into a garment. When it all works the entire process is enjoyable.*

How would you describe your creative process? *I start in the Royal College library, where I stay for hours just doing research, and then in the studio, which I don't leave for months. Eventually a collection is born.*

How would you define contemporary fashion? *Contemporary fashion is something that is modern. I suppose modern is defined by relevance, and the fact it simply feels right.*

Who or what informs your work? *Everything, I am a magpie. I am informed by my eyes and by my ears.*

www.erdem.co.uk

1. Jacquard gilet, silk vest and harem trousers in flower cluster print, S/S 08. **2–5.** Full-length lace gown; fluted-sleeve taffeta cocktail dress with lace bodice; hand embroidered moth-print cocktail dress; lace-paneled taffeta shift dress. All A/W 07. **6.** Short dress with lace tights, S/S 07.

6

1

2

3

'I want every single piece to have its own identity and to always be masculine,' states French designer Eric Lebon. Born in the West Indies and described as a self-trained designer, Lebon is inspired by hip-hop and urban culture with a nod towards traditional styles. He made his debut presentation in 2007 at the Paris Men's Fashion Week after being selected for the twenty-first Festival International des Arts de la Mode at Hyères.

Eric Lebon——*34/100*

'I don't claim to be unique, but I know that I have a style a little different from the other designers that come from the same generation, thanks to some details and also to a different idea of menswear,' explains Lebon. He aims to bring something new to menswear by not sticking to the tendencies and elements that already exist, or by converting women's clothing to men's clothing. 'I just want men to have their own pieces and identity, as women do,' he says.

Lebon works against the common ideals of male beauty and identity that are put forward by many fashion magazines and designers. He wants to give men who desire it the opportunity to find in their wardrobe beautiful and detailed clothing designed and made specifically for them.

When designing, Lebon does not have a specific topic in mind for a collection, preferring not to be restrained or prevented from exploring other ideas. He believes both the process and the product are integral to the success of his collections. 'I start with a series of drawings according to my desires. Then, progressively, the identity of the collection emerges, and then the sketches and my wishes evolve with my model-making and in the choice of fabrics and the technical rules. As I'm a perfectionist, I don't leave any details to chance,' he admits.

For Lebon, fashion design is not an artistic expression. He attempts to dissociate notions of art and fashion, even though he recognizes that there are some similarities in the processes. His ambition is to allow men the opportunity to have the freedom of choice through his masculine and wearable clothes.

www.ericlebon.com

1–3. Patchwork sleeveless hoodies, S/S 05. **4.** Striped cotton turban with plastic shirt, S/S 08. **5.** Black, grey and white cotton sweater with skull print, A/W 04. **6–9.** Oversized wool jacket with high-waisted trousers; handknit cardigan with deconstructed cotton shirt; grey handknit leggings; sleeveless handknit vest with fur. 21st International festival in Hyères. **10.** Cotton print scarf, S/S 05. **11.** Grey cotton sweater with blue sun design, S/S 05.

'I just want men to have their own pieces and identity, as women do'___Eric Lebon

11

10

1

2

Twin sisters Annette and Daniela Felder left their native Germany in 2002 to work for British designers Robert Cary-Williams and Stephen Jones, before going on to study at Central Saint Martins. Annette studied fashion communication and worked for *i-D* magazine, while Daniela, who studied fashion and print design, focused on creating collections. Combining their different skills, the design duo set up their womenswear line, Felder · Felder, while still studying at college. They graduated in 2006 and were immediately selected by Gen Art to show their collection during New York Fashion Week.

Felder · Felder—*35/100*

The label quickly won the attention of the international press and soon developed a strong following. Collections feature dresses in the sisters' signature silk fabrics that are finished with details such as leather trimming or metal buckles, creating an edgy but feminine look. 'We always aim to create a look for a strong woman who isn't afraid to show her feminine side as well. As twin sisters we know all too well about contrasts that complement each other or in fact need each other to make the whole thing work, and this is reflected in our designs by mixing contrasting elements.'

The twins tend to be visually inspired and excited by anything from a rock concert to their mother's wardrobe or old photographs. They take the inspiration, deconstruct it and balance it with a contrast, which they feel will make it complete. 'The next step is to make the whole thing work as a collection and to make it look modern', they enthuse. 'Then there is a quiet time where the two of us work on different design ideas that we then bring together. Our ideas usually work against each other, which we like. It allows a subtle disharmony to appear in the story.'

Contemporary fashion, according to *Felder · Felder*, is concerned with embracing a modern feel, which is elegant and exciting at the same time. They consider trashiness to be dated as quality is key to their work.

www.felderfelder.com

1. Silk-crepe shift with leggings, A/W 06. **2.** Shift dress with metallic embellishment, A/W 07. **3.** Polaroids from A/W 06 shoot. **4–7.** Leather and chiffon jewellery; chiffon dress with jewellery neckline; chiffon cocktail dress with patent jacket; printed chiffon dress. All S/S 07. **8.** T-shirt and leggings, A/W 06. **9.** Silk-crepe shift with studded neckline, A/W 07.

3

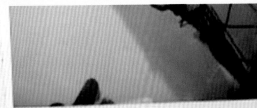

4

5

6

7

*'Our ideas usually work against each other, which we like. It allows a subtle disharmony to appear in the story'*___Felder · Felder

8

9

Born in the Portuguese Azores, Felipe Oliveira Baptista grew up in Lisbon. He left Portugal at the age of 18 to study fashion design at Kingston University in London. On graduation, he worked for Max Mara and Cerutti before becoming Christophe Lemaire's design assistant.

Felipe Oliveira Baptista
____*36/100*

Baptista won the Fashion Award at the 2002 Festival International des Arts de la Mode in Hyères and the coveted ANDAM award in 2003, the year that proved to be his breakthrough. In the same year he set up his own label with his Parisian wife Séverine and launched his luxury ready-to-wear collection during the Paris couture shows, becoming the first Portuguese designer to be a guest on the haute couture calendar.

How would you define your aesthetic? *Constructed, graphic, bold and somehow pure.*

What is the most enjoyable part of design? *Everything. But if I must choose then the research part is extremely enjoyable because at that stage anything is possible.*

How would you describe your customer? *I tend not to think of one 'customer'. I like the idea that in each collection there are pieces that suit both 30-year-old and 60-year-old women, regardless of their size. I do like to think that customers appreciate quality and pay attention to cut, details and comfort.*

How would you describe your creative process? *Each season I work around a different story or concept. It can start with words, an idea or a mixture of references. For a month I research and develop the story so that when the design process starts each garment is part of the story, both a main character and background.*

How would you define contemporary fashion? *Garments that somehow translate our times.*

Who or what informs your work? *It depends on the season. It can be as varied as dinosaurs, horses, anatomy, Mexican wrestlers, an artist, my own photographs or a particular garment.*

What is the most challenging aspect of design? *To achieve the right balance between an idea and a wearable garment.*

www.felipeoliveirabaptista.com

1. Functional ball dress, A/W 06. **2-5.** White 'Terminator' suit; 'Super Spike' leggings with vest; 'Green Jaguar' cocktail dress; 'Orange Flame' tunic with cropped jacket. All 'les Catcheuses', S/S 08. **6.** Black trench, A/W 06.

6

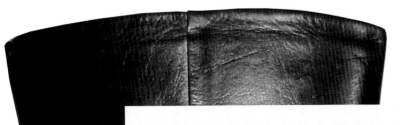

Julia Lundsten was born in Finland and studied at the Royal College of Art in London. After undertaking an MA in fashion womenswear, she went on to study footwear, graduating in 2003. She won the Manolo Blahník Award in 2002, and in 2003 she launched her first own-brand collection for Spring/Summer 05.

Finsk____37/100

Describe your design philosophy. *A designer should never go for the safe option; it is really important to take risks and try new things. Unforeseen outcomes when experimenting can help create the best designs.*

How would you define your aesthetic? *Modern, but in some ways traditional. Clean, strong lines but still with a sensitive beauty. I like high-quality materials – a material itself can be a design if used in the right way.*

What is the most enjoyable part of design? *Designing. When I can play with materials and shapes, imagining the product as it will become. From sketching to working drawings and material selection up until the prototypes are made is the best part.*

How would you describe your customer? *Intelligent, always looking for something different and new. Many of our customers are architects or designers.*

How would you define contemporary fashion? *Interesting and fun. There are a lot of good designers and designs around; however, their work is very hard to find in shops as I think buyers often choose the safe before the new and exciting, which is a shame.*

Who or what informs your work? *The architects and furniture designers in Finland from the 1920s to the 1940s who were doing something completely different and new. They were using materials in a new way; shapes were brave and new. Nature and architecture in general are big inspirations, as well as different cultures and places. I am very curious and I never stop reading.*

www.finsk.com

1. Promotional postcard design, S/S 07. **2.** Black leather wedge with wooden heel, A/W 07. **3.** Black leather 'double boot', A/W 07. **4.** Zigzag t-bar shoes, A/W 06. **5.** White and bronze leather ankle boot, A/W 06. **6.** Black and bronze leather asymmetric ankle boot, A/W 06. **7–8.** Stills from 'Framed' animation, A/W 06.

3

*'A designer should never go for the safe option; it is really important to take risks and try new things'*__**Finsk**

5

4

6

7

8

1

2

German Frank Leder is a champion of creating wearable and quirky menswear garments that have strong roots in traditional clothing design. Graduating from Central Saint Martins, he showed his menswear collections in Paris in 2002. The same year, Leder returned to Berlin to celebrate his German identity and to create clothes that would be a product of his local design environment.

Frank Leder___*38/100*

Describe your design philosophy. *High-quality garments that recall a Germany of the past, with a surprising modernity at its core. Garments that are part of a bigger picture, which settle into a given story. Garments that reflect a certain intellectual humour in their context.*

How would you define your aesthetic? *A Germany from the past for a modern setting. And a humorous, intellectual approach. A grounded down-to-earth thinking with an unconventional way of working and perceiving.*

What is the most enjoyable part of design? *To see an abstract idea being transformed into a wearable and striking garment.*

How would you describe your customer? *Every person who wants to walk a certain route and path with me and my offerings. Those who want to open a new door and are prepared to discover.*

How would you describe your creative process? *Images and ideas that filter through my system are being transformed into grounded goods. Garments settle into a world, which is defined by my own photographed aesthetic and artistry.*

How would you define successful menswear? *It should be rooted in a strong design language. It should show its own character and where it is coming from. The identification with the garment is important, as well as a certain aspect of discovery and intellectual stimulation.*

www.frank-leder.com

1. 'Pay Attention', A/W 03. 2. 'Hinterland 1, Erz', A/W 07. 3. Studio detail shot. Iron ball and chain from 'Break that Vicious Circle', A/W 05. 4. Portrait of Frank Leder. 5–8. Free work, 'Der Weg der Kartoffel', showing garments from 'Grey Wolves', A/W 06. 9. Jacket and tie-front trousers, 'Afrika', S/S 07, modelled by artist Martin Eder. 10. Garments from A/W 07.

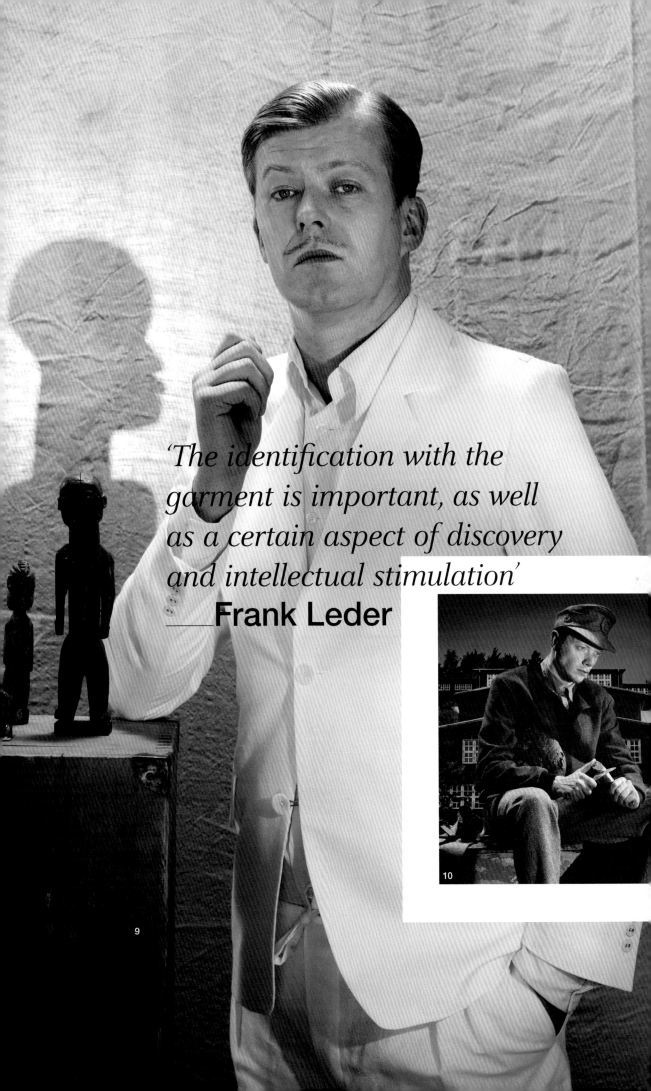

'The identification with the garment is important, as well as a certain aspect of discovery and intellectual stimulation'
___Frank Leder

9

10

1

2

Armenian-Lebanese designer Garen Demerdjian founded Gardem in Paris in 2002. After studying art and painting in his home country of Lebanon, Demerdjian moved with his family to Greece to escape the turmoil of the civil war. His paintings were shown at several prominent galleries in Greece, and after the war he returned to Beirut to attend the Academie des Beaux Arts, graduating in 1996.

Gardem___*39/100*

After leaving art school, Demerdjian enrolled at ESMOD (Ecole de Mode Internationale) in Paris and graduated with a degree in fashion design in 1999. In 2004, two years after starting his label, he formed a partnership with Bedie Moran, an international business strategist, to develop the Gardem brand.

Demerdjian started to get noticed, and won the New Generation Award for his Spring/ Summer 05 collection, receiving sponsorship for his first catwalk show in London from the British Fashion Council and the UK fashion chain Topshop. More recently, he was the recipient of the Innovation in Design Award from Cotton USA for his Spring/Summer 07 collection.

It is very important to Demerdjian to design luxurious fashions that give women the opportunity to create a style that is unique and personalized, putting together his easy pieces in their own individual way. He describes his aesthetic as 'minimal and decorative at the same time'.

Using a monochromatic palette, Demerdjian selects colours that are soft on the eye and have a strong basis in nature, and he works largely with blacks and neutrals. He has developed a signature style that is carefully structured but designed to create the appearance of effortless fluidity through layering and asymmetric detail. He lists music, the forms of nature, modern art and the shapes of the eighteenth century as informing his work.

www.gardem.net

1. Crepe-silk knitted top and pants, A/W 07. 2. Wool gloves with metallic accessories, A/W 05. 3. Silk-jersey dress with ruffles, S/S 08. 4–6. Long silk dress with printed chiffon underskirt; floral garland; gauze dress with all-over flowers. All S/S 08. 7. Silk and velvet dress, sleeveless silk top with long train, hat and long leather boots, A/W 07. 8. Embellished knitted gloves, A/W 05.

3

'Minimal and decorative at the same time'___Gardem

7

8

1

2

3

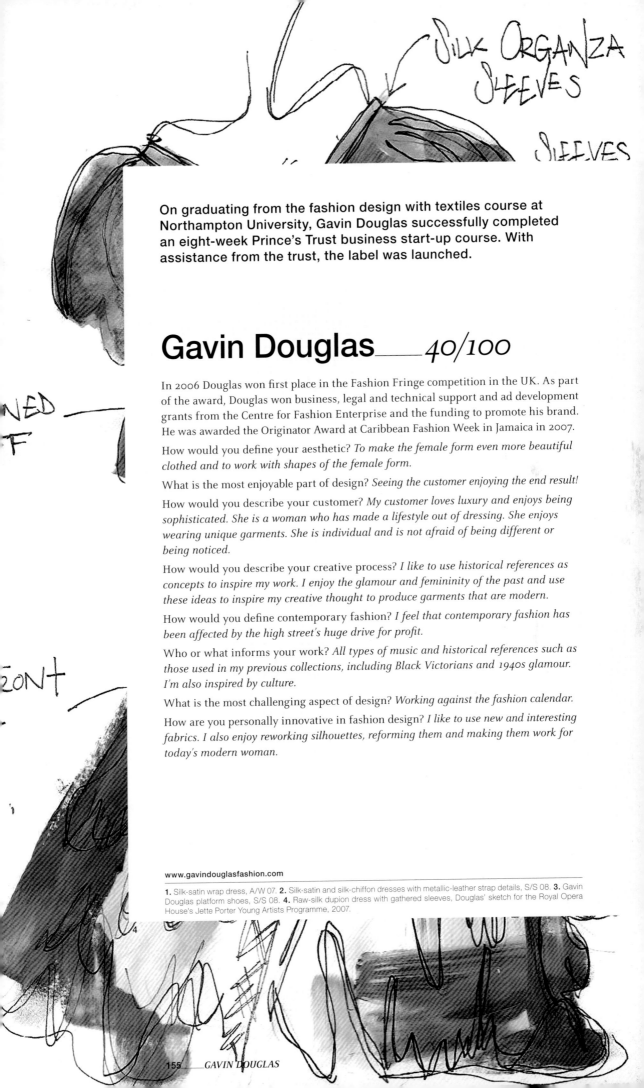

On graduating from the fashion design with textiles course at Northampton University, Gavin Douglas successfully completed an eight-week Prince's Trust business start-up course. With assistance from the trust, the label was launched.

Gavin Douglas___40/100

In 2006 Douglas won first place in the Fashion Fringe competition in the UK. As part of the award, Douglas won business, legal and technical support and ad development grants from the Centre for Fashion Enterprise and the funding to promote his brand. He was awarded the Originator Award at Caribbean Fashion Week in Jamaica in 2007.

How would you define your aesthetic? *To make the female form even more beautiful clothed and to work with shapes of the female form.*

What is the most enjoyable part of design? *Seeing the customer enjoying the end result!*

How would you describe your customer? *My customer loves luxury and enjoys being sophisticated. She is a woman who has made a lifestyle out of dressing. She enjoys wearing unique garments. She is individual and is not afraid of being different or being noticed.*

How would you describe your creative process? *I like to use historical references as concepts to inspire my work. I enjoy the glamour and femininity of the past and use these ideas to inspire my creative thought to produce garments that are modern.*

How would you define contemporary fashion? *I feel that contemporary fashion has been affected by the high street's huge drive for profit.*

Who or what informs your work? *All types of music and historical references such as those used in my previous collections, including Black Victorians and 1940s glamour. I'm also inspired by culture.*

What is the most challenging aspect of design? *Working against the fashion calendar.*

How are you personally innovative in fashion design? *I like to use new and interesting fabrics. I also enjoy reworking silhouettes, reforming them and making them work for today's modern woman.*

www.gavindouglasfashion.com

1. Silk-satin wrap dress, A/W 07. **2.** Silk-satin and silk-chiffon dresses with metallic-leather strap details, S/S 08. **3.** Gavin Douglas platform shoes, S/S 08. **4.** Raw-silk dupion dress with gathered sleeves, Douglas' sketch for the Royal Opera House's Jette Porter Young Artists Programme, 2007.

1

2

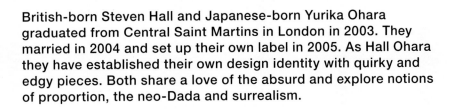

British-born Steven Hall and Japanese-born Yurika Ohara graduated from Central Saint Martins in London in 2003. They married in 2004 and set up their own label in 2005. As Hall Ohara they have established their own design identity with quirky and edgy pieces. Both share a love of the absurd and explore notions of proportion, the neo-Dada and surrealism.

Hall Ohara___ *41/100*

As a starting point for their designs, *Hall Ohara* use very commercial garments and then try to incorporate surreal elements. They explain, 'Our dreams inspire us, but financial restraints inform us.' Hall and Ohara use different techniques to create their signature prints, fusing glamour and rock and roll with a Japanese quirkiness.

Winners of the Fashion Council and Topshop's New Generation designers award in 2006, the duo have continued to develop their unique aesthetic; their striking and playful designs are a mixture of rock chick and geek chic, combining exaggerated proportions with bold prints and unusual embellishments. Underlying all of their collections is an unmistakable sly sense of humour.

The *Hall Ohara* silhouette often shatters preconceived ideas as the designers employ creative cutting techniques to communicate their vision of fashion design. The influential style press, including *i-D* Magazine, *Dazed & Confused Japan*, *Nylon* and *Amelia's Magazine*, has supported this distinctive approach to fashion.

www.hallohara.com

1–2. Wool jersey dress with hand-knitted edging; striped taffeta and wool jersey dress. Both A/W 06. **3.** Print design by Yurika Ohara, hand drawn with a Japanese calligraphy brush, A/W 07. **4–5.** Clown-print silk dress; clown-print silk shirt. S/S 06. **6–9.** Photoshoot for *Dazed & Confused Japan* for their red clothing issue.

3

'Our dreams inspire us, but financial restraints inform us'
___**Hall Ohara**

4

5

7

8

9

1

2

German designers Kathleen Waibel, Carmen Boch, Alexa Frueh and Peter Koenig founded HALTBAR in 2001. The purpose of the collaboration was to create designs for interiors, textiles and accessories. The German word 'haltbar' describes something that is lasting, durable and solid. This definition applies to the design collective and to the spirit of its work: the designers' primary aim is to create something that is long lasting and high-quality, timeless but also modern.

HALTBAR___*42/100*

Underlying their design philosophy is a decision to work with family and handicraft businesses to use and preserve existing infrastructures and knowledge and to present a modern interpretation of traditional products.

In 2003 *HALTBAR MURKUDIS*, a collaboration between Kathleen Waibel, Peter Koenig and Greek designer Kostas Murkudis, was launched. Remaining true to the philosophy behind *HALTBAR*, they created a unisex clothing collection based on German workwear and designed to embody functionality and comfort.

How would you define your aesthetic? *Straight, clean, timeless, relaxed and cool.*

What is the most enjoyable part of design? *To do what you want to and what you are convinced of. To gain the attention of people who understand and appreciate your philosophy.*

How would you describe your customer? *People who have developed their own style over the years. People who are self-confident about themselves and their style. People who want to wear clothes that underline their personality.*

How would you describe your creative process? *It's a very conceptual approach. We conduct research, especially into workwear, and adapt and redefine pieces for the fashion market.*

How would you define contemporary fashion? *Something that has a contemporary as well as a durable and long-lasting style.*

Who or what informs your work? *People, communication, tradition, culture and nature.*

What is the most challenging aspect of design? *To remain true to oneself and one's principles. To create things that match both the zeitgeist and the philosophy that functions in everyday life.*

www.haltbar.de

1. Cotton pants vintaged with oil, S/S 05. 2. Loden wool pants with leather bag, A/W 07. 3. Knitwear, A/W 05. 4. Wool blanket, A/W 03. 5–8. Women's cotton trench; merino wool troyer; men's cotton trench; two-zip pants with reversible cashmere sweater. A/W 05. 9. Fitted shirt and relaxed trousers, A/W 03. 10. First collection displayed in a Berlin store, A/W 03.

3

5

4

7

8

10

'*Straight, clean, timeless, relaxed and cool*'____**HALTBAR**

9

1

2

Born in South Africa, Hamish Morrow moved to London in 1989 to study fashion at Central Saint Martins, after which he completed his studies at the Royal College of Art, obtaining an MA in menswear fashion design. After graduation, he worked for the Italian label Byblos under the creative direction of John Bartlett.

Hamish Morrow___*43/100*

Returning to London in 2000, Morrow began to work on his own label, which he launched during London Fashion Week in 2001. Over the following three years he divided his time between London, where his own line was generating critical acclaim, and consultancy posts abroad, which included working on couture at Louis Feraud, on menswear at Fendi and alongside Mariuccia Mandelli at Krizia.

Morrow defines his particular philosophy as being to 'observe the world we live in and reflect it by responding to and anticipating lifestyle changes,' believing that 'the most modern clothes are those that address societal developments and changes and provide a wardrobe for people's changing needs'.

For Morrow, his customer requires clothing that is versatile, comfortable, luxurious and that travels well. He believes his clients have a clear sense of self and personal style and love clothes and the way they can enhance life's experiences. Fashion, according to Morrow, is 'eclectic, something for everyone: often irrelevant, not always creative, sometimes brilliant'.

The difficulties of running a company caused Morrow to withdraw from the fashion week calendar for four seasons, during which time he searched for business support. This resulted in the launch of his commercially successful luxury sportswear collection in 2005. Using a combination of sports and luxury fabrics with nanotechnology, the line focuses on essential pieces that have effortless style.

The most enjoyable part of design for Morrow is to have the seed of an idea and to nurture and develop it, which 'enriches the mind and soul and provides the energy to continue'. He sees the creative process as taking place completely inside his head – 'When it's ready, out it comes on to paper and cloth' – and believes his greatest challenge as a designer is to create a beautiful product that has a clear and relevant use.

www.hamishmorrow.com

1. Cashmere draped cardigan with silk lamé trousers, A/W 06. 2. Parachute-web tape top, A/W 03. 3. Jeans embellished with NASA gold 'space blanket' material, 'Fashion at Zero Gravity' project, 2005. 4-7. Garments in silk and satin, S/S 06. 8. Draped viscose-jersey blouson, S/S 08. 9. Silk twill dress with digitally-projected virtual print .

4

6

7

'The most modern clothes are those that address societal developments and changes and provide a wardrobe for people's changing needs' ___**Hamish Morrow**

1

Graduating with a degree in fine art from Manchester University in 1990, Heather Blake went on to teach art and design for ten years in London and Hong Kong. In 2002 Blake decided to leave Hong Kong and return to London to study footwear design and production at Cordwainers at London College of Fashion. Blake worked for a year at bespoke shoemakers Foster & Son, where she learned the craft of shoemaking. She then studied for an MA in footwear design at the Royal College of Art between 2004 and 2006. In 2006 Blake won Accessories Collection of the Year at ITS#5 in Trieste, Italy. The prize involved producing a new collection, which was shown at ITS#6 in 2007, on which she collaborated with Italian shoemaker Salvatore Ferragamo.

Heather Blake___44/100

Describe your design philosophy. *Perpetual motion: experimentation, discovery and the creative process. The idea that the journey is the destination.*

How would you define your aesthetic? *Industrial Baroque.*

What is the most enjoyable part of design? *The research and experimentation.*

How would you describe your customer? *A confident, quite flamboyant woman, someone like Alison Goldfrapp or Dita Von Teese.*

How would you describe your creative process? *A continual cycle of creation and destruction: intense, traumatic and all-consuming.*

How would you define contemporary fashion? *Thank God there are innovators and extremists out there to save us all from mediocrity.*

Who or what informs your work? *The relationship between art and science, tradition and technology. Also, aerospace, nature, Luigi Colani, film noir and surrealism.*

What is the most challenging aspect of design? *You can design anything you want on paper; making it is the tough part.*

How are you personally innovative in fashion design? *This is a question that I would avoid asking myself, as in doing so I would put myself under such enormous pressure to achieve a 'modern' or 'innovative' outcome, which would never be modern or innovative enough. It would negate the reason I design, which is for the joy of it.*

www.heatherblake.co.uk

1. 'Lacrima' black suede peep-toe with silver heel, S/S 07. 2. 'Twist' peep-toe court, S/S 06. 3. 'Maria' black suede sandal with cut-out wedge heel and silver accessories, S/S 06. 4. 'Paloma' light blue leather pump with opanka sole, S/S 07.

2

'A continual cycle of creation and
destruction: intense, traumatic
and all-consuming'
____Heather Blake

Henrik Vibskov grew up in the countryside of Jutland in Denmark. He worked as a creative in the visual arts, encompassing both film and music and exhibiting in Denmark, France, Germany and Japan. Believing that creativity can be channelled into any medium, Vibskov decided to focus on fashion design, and in 1996 he was a finalist in the Smirnoff International Fashion Awards. From this success he went to work for Danish fashion label Bruuns Bazaar.

Henrik Vibskov——*45/100*

After studying at the Hillevi Van Deurs design school in Copenhagen, Vibskov decided to challenge his fashion ideology and he enrolled at Central Saint Martins in London in 1998. He graduated in 2001 and received a vast amount of media interest from style magazines.

On launching his menswear collection, Vibskov was picked up by a number of trendsetting stores such as Colette in Paris, The Pineal Eye in London, Midwest in Tokyo and Traffik in Moscow. He is a regular at Men's Fashion Week in Paris, where he is known for his innovative, colourful and eclectic menswear.

Describe your design philosophy. *It has a very laid-back feeling – 3D colours with a sharp and technical line.*

What is the most enjoyable part of design? *Making it up and creating the installation show.*

How would you describe your customer? *I thought they were young, but actually I have grandmothers buying one of my dresses, because it was named 'the grand mum dress'.*

How would you describe your creative process? *It is very slow in the beginning and suddenly too fast. Last minute dot com but still in focus, I hope.*

How would you define contemporary fashion? *Something that can fit into modern life and still work after 10 years.*

What is the most challenging aspect of design? *To get from ideas to how the look finally works. Sometimes my brain visualizes something differently than in real life, but I get better with age, I think. Normally I say 90% of ideas are shit, 5% are good and 5% tip-top.*

www.henrikvibskov.com

1. Short suit with checked scarf, 'The Fantabulous Bicycle Music Factory', S/S 08. **2.** Brights and geometrics, 'The Black Carrots' A/W 07. **3.** Installation at the A/W 06 'Cyklys' show. **4–5.** Garments from 'Toti', A/W 05. **6–9.** Layering at 'Big Wet Shiny Boobies', S/S 07. **10.** Printed wrap, A/W 05.

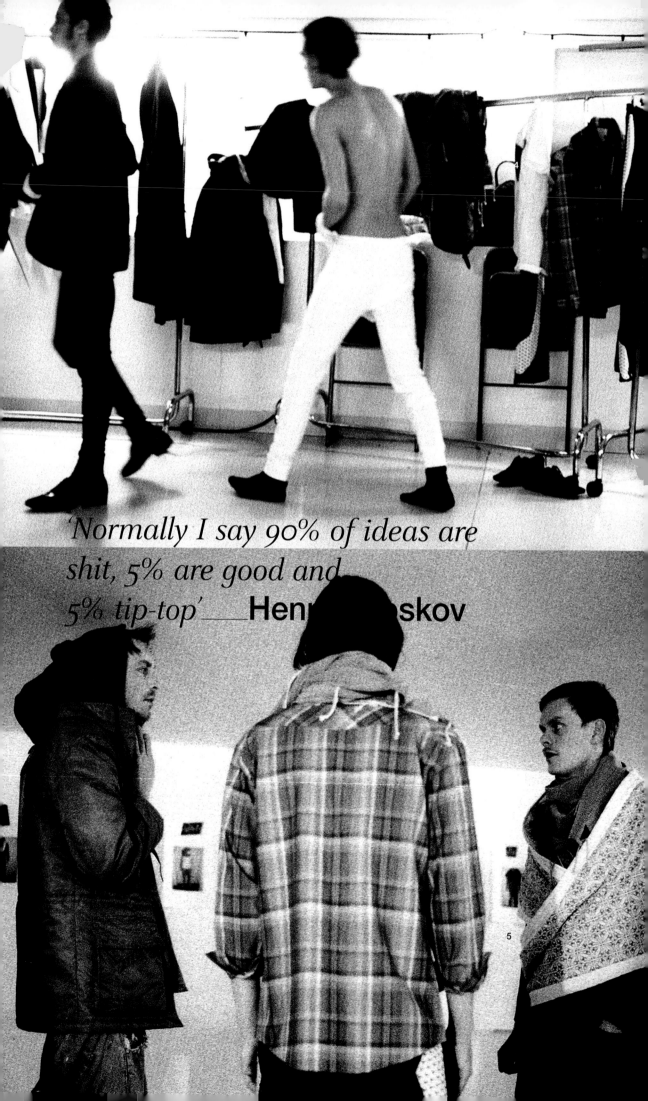

'Normally I say 90% of ideas are shit, 5% are good and 5% tip-top'___Henr██ ███skov

1

Central Saint Martins graduates Adam Entwistle and Emma Hales comprise Horace. Illustrator Philip Grisewood also forms part of the Horace team, and his designs can be found on the label's t-shirts. The line was first launched during London Fashion Week in September 2001.

Horace___*46/100*

According to the team, *Horace* is a continuous work in progress. Their philosophy is to create a collection, which overall or piece by piece can be identified by its long-standing aesthetic. 'We mainly like to reference things from a lowbrow or juvenile sentiment. Fast food, music, horror, anything disposable that affects the continually changing culture of need and collectability.'

Aesthetically *Horace* is 'dark', not only because of the prominent use of black but also because of the silhouettes, textures and subdued prints that keep the collection looking sinister. *Horace* is popular in Japan and with European club kids: 'Our customer is more of a stand-off person, possibly someone who could be described as having an underdog syndrome, which is a contradiction in terms based on the fact that they obviously like to be odd and stand out.'

For the team, designing is a collaborative and social process. 'We spend a lot of time joking around, doodling and hanging out drinking coffee. We love to watch people and mainly that's where we like to see ideas or how we come up with ideas. Artwork is influenced by almost anything you can think of – watching television is the biggest influence or looking at the pictures in magazines, shop windows and tube stations.' Sci-fi literature, film, computer and video games and graphic design also inspire them. 'We try to stay true to our real tastes and stay interested in all the things that we were originally informed and inspired by. As we get older, we continually grow and bend as those tastes change slightly. So it's a case of seeing the same references in trend and youth culture being reinterpreted and remoulded by younger and more excited people.'

www.myspace.com/horace_tv

1. 'Beetlejuice' long-sleeve trench, A/W 06. 2. 'Brainwashed' t-shirt with white platform shoes, S/S 06. 3. Straight-edge t-shirt with burgundy jeans, A/W 06. 4. Doubled-up trench coats with washed twisted-leather boots, A/W 07. 5. Panel shirt with leather Teddy-boy jacket and handmade converse-style leather high-tops, A/W 06. 6. Airbrushed bleached skull top and tulle tutu dress, A/W 07. 7. Dip-dyed rayon handknit, bleached jeans and custom high-tops, A/W 07.

3

'We love to watch people and mainly that's where we like to see ideas or how we come up with ideas'——**Horace**

6

7

1

2

Greek-born Ioannis Dimitrousis graduated from the London College of Fashion in 2005 and presented his first collection at London Graduate Fashion Week. This provided the designer with his first opportunity to showcase his experimental designs, which combine unexpected fabrics and decorative effects created by reworking the beading and crochet work of his native country.

Ioannis Dimitrousis___47/100

Dimitrousis's trademark look brings the spirit of high fashion to traditional textile work. His innovative and imaginative use of materials has brought him to the attention of established designers and has led to him working with Louis de Gama, Jonathan Saunders and Roland Mouret. In 2006 Dimitrousis's professional catwalk debut was held during the 'On/Off' schedule event at London Fashion Week and attracted acclaim from the worldwide fashion press.

Describe your design philosophy. *Traditional with a versatile slant that makes it futuristic.*

How would you define your aesthetic? *Bold, dynamic, a mixture of textures and fabrics, versatile. 'Fashionista' with moments of 'chav', a bit rude or emotional, a confusion of feelings and question marks with naturalistic aspects.*

What is the most enjoyable part of design? *The moment when the designs come to life and I realize that they are not just designs and sketches but they can also be wearable garments.*

How would you define contemporary fashion? *There is a futuristic feeling at the moment in the fashion industry, but it is too aware of what the consumer wants and there is not much originality and experimentation. Many big fashion houses become repetitive and boring with their main and diffusion lines: they prefer an easy way to make more profit and avoid creativity and risk-taking. It is mostly new designers who create the trends.*

Who or what informs your work? *All of the five senses. What I see and hear, anything that I smell and taste and whatever I touch.*

What is the most challenging aspect of design? *To find the balance between the customer's needs and the originality of my designs.*

www.ioannisdimitrousis.com

1. Silk printed vest and silk jumpsuit with tassels, S/S 07. 2. Organic wool crochet jumper, organic denim jeans and digitally-printed hand accessory, A/W 07. 3. Materials and fabric samples from S/S 07 and A/W 07. 4. Organic silk one-button jacket with embroidery and bondage, organic silk crochet vest with recycled glass beads, S/S 07. 5. Organic wool scarves, silk-wool jacket with pearl beadwork embroidery worn with patchwork skirt, graduate collection, A/W 05. 6. Organic jackets and scarves from A/W 06 worn all together.

3

'Traditional with a versatile slant
that makes it futuristic'
Ioannis Dimitrousis

4

5

6

1

2

3

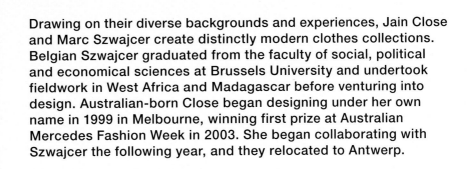

Drawing on their diverse backgrounds and experiences, Jain Close and Marc Szwajcer create distinctly modern clothes collections. Belgian Szwajcer graduated from the faculty of social, political and economical sciences at Brussels University and undertook fieldwork in West Africa and Madagascar before venturing into design. Australian-born Close began designing under her own name in 1999 in Melbourne, winning first prize at Australian Mercedes Fashion Week in 2003. She began collaborating with Szwajcer the following year, and they relocated to Antwerp.

Jain Close/Marc Szwajcer
___48/100

In 2005 the label *Jain Close/Marc Szwajcer* was launched with a lean, anti-nostalgic Spring/Summer collection with an industrial twist. 'We think we are both practical and methodological at the same time. We try to keep up with our convictions without losing track of the reality that surrounds us,' they explain. Successfully combining a minimalist aesthetic and precise cutting, both designers embrace a philosophy of 'less is more' with regard to shape and colour.

Their aesthetic appears strikingly minimal, but the results are achieved through a defined method of working: 'We work by reduction,' they state. 'We reduce our designs out of the need to keep a balance and honesty, erring towards less rather than more. It's about how we can function together as a team, and also about the need to stop at the point where we find a balance between ourselves and the object.'

Close and Szwajcer's approach to design is very practical. 'We work closely with pattern and fabrication rather than illustration. For us the fit of a garment, the cut, practicality, functionality and movement are integral to our aesthetic. In this way each and every garment is worn during the design process, which makes them dynamic and enduring.'

The designers will not attempt to define or judge contemporary style, believing it is 'irremediably rooted in time, culture, society, economy and other factors that we do not want to get lost in'. Instead they allow four disciplines to shape their work – focus, balance, function and structure – and in the process create unashamedly contemporary clothes.

www.jcms.be

1. Cotton and cashmere fine jersey dress, S/S 06. **2-3.** Cotton twill swing coat and polyamide elastane dress, S/S 07 show. **4.** Pattern-making room in the Antwerp studio. **5.** Polyester crepe trench, A/W 06. **6–9.** Cotton twill jacket and coat with fine jersey dress, S/S 06.

'We reduce our designs out of the need to keep a balance and honesty, erring towards less rather than more'
___Jain Close/Marc Sawajcer

Dutchman Jan Taminiau graduated from Arnhem Academy of Art in 2001, going on to study at the Fashion Institute Arnhem from where he graduated in 2003. While still a student, he sold one of his fashion creations to the Municipal Museum in The Hague. His final-year project earned him the prestigious Roos Gesink Award for the most talented designer. Taminiau has undertaken work experience at Olivier Theyskens, Oscar Süleyman and Hubert Barrère in Paris (corsetier for Dior, Yves Saint Laurent and Madonna). In 2003 he launched his own label, JANTAMINIAU.

JANTAMINIAU___49/100

'The basis of my work is always the same,' explains Taminiau. 'I am continually translating the asymmetrical mirror of life. Everything I undertake in daily life, I place in my own context. This is reflected in my work, the 2D/3D concept and my love of technique and craftsmanship.' Inspired by materials, craft and techniques, Taminiau gathers information from books, documentaries and museums, such as the Dutch Textile Museum. He inherits his love of nostalgia from his family who are antique dealers and interior designers.

The starting point for Taminiau's designs is a flat swathe of fabric. 'This two-dimensional surface unfolds into a stylish three-dimensional fashion creation. The symbolism inherent in the process of unfolding (the gestures, unwrapping a gift, transformation from caterpillar to butterfly), the seizure of these moments, the sentiment evoked by unwrapping and the eventual emergence of the consummate feminine creations, come together in a subtle and refined end result.'

In his search for new forms, Taminiau enables the wearer to experiment with form through his meticulously constructed creations. He explains: 'In my quest for the perfect fit I pursue new shapes and unconventional techniques. By weaving and interweaving fabrics I enable a natural form to emerge, which draws character from the wearer.' Taminiau's aesthetic is inherently feminine, romantic, nostalgic and sculptural.

www.jantaminiau.com

1. Red silk-chiffon bonbon dress, '1, 2, 3, 4', A/W 06. **2.** Crepe-de-chine dress embroidered with antique beads and Swarovski crystals, 'Postbag', S/S 05. **3–6.** Tulle dress with wool boucle underskirt; handpainted silk-chiffon dress embellished with Swarovski crystals with underskirt inspired by cricket leg-guards; ivory silk dress covered with dress made from beach-chair fabric; tulle underskirt covered with antique-lace dress. All 'Radical Chic', S/S 07. **7.** Fitted inner-dress covered with silk-organza balloon-shaped dress with antique-metal ribbon, 'Empire', A/W 05.

2

3

'I am continually translating the asymmetrical mirror of life'
___JANTAMINIAU

5

6

2

1

4

5

Born in the UK, Jean-Pierre Braganza grew up in Canada where he studied fine art. Moving back to London to study fashion at Central Saint Martins, Braganza worked for Robert Cary-Williams whilst still at college. After graduation, he assisted Roland Mouret where he refined his tailoring skills. He presented his first own-name collection in Milan in 2003.

Jean-Pierre Braganza
50/100

Braganza's design philosophy is based on his obsession with the human form and his expertly cut patterns accentuate body shapes. Against this, he contrasts unexpected detailing, which is often compact yet still functional. 'I fuse illusory patternmaking with sartorial fundamentalism while manipulating historical ideas and embracing futurism,' explains Braganza.

The designer's aesthetic leans towards the dark side of the imagination. 'I like to listen to hard rock, industrial and techno music. I love black, and my designs are almost always imagined in black. I'm always trying to learn and am fascinated with history and philosophy. My style has frequently been called "rock and roll", and I agree with this in the sense that rock music is subversive, empirically jarring and intensely ecstatic.'

Manipulating convention and subverting traditions sums up Braganza's approach to design. Naturally occurring twists, folds and proportions of clothing are forced into permanence through his designs. He enjoys draping and designing on the body and although he finds pattern-cutting on the table rewarding, for him, there is nothing like playing with shapes on the body.

Braganza cites many inspirations, including Matthew Barney, H.R. Giger, Thierry Mugler, Trent Reznor from Nine Inch Nails and David Bowie. He begins his creative process with drawing. 'As an illustrator, I begin with the skeleton, adding flesh and then adding clothing as another layer to the human form,' he explains. 'I exaggerate and manipulate this "extra skin" into pleasing shapes and unconventional proportions. I then add conventional details but with a twist, moulding them to suit my imagination of the moment. I use the golden ratio as a tool for creating form, and sometimes warp the ratio, which can create beauty by discordance.'

www.jeanpierrebraganza.com

1. Peach sateen shirt with shoulder flaps and hip pleat worn with 3/4 length trousers, S/S 08. **2–5.** Bleached denim asymmetric jeans with two-way gathered-sleeve coat; brocade 3/4 length trousers with handknit oversized wool cardigan; leather capelet with asymmetric jeans; two-way stretch sailor trousers and pleated waistcoat. A/W 06. **6.** 'Spine' print, S/S 08.

6

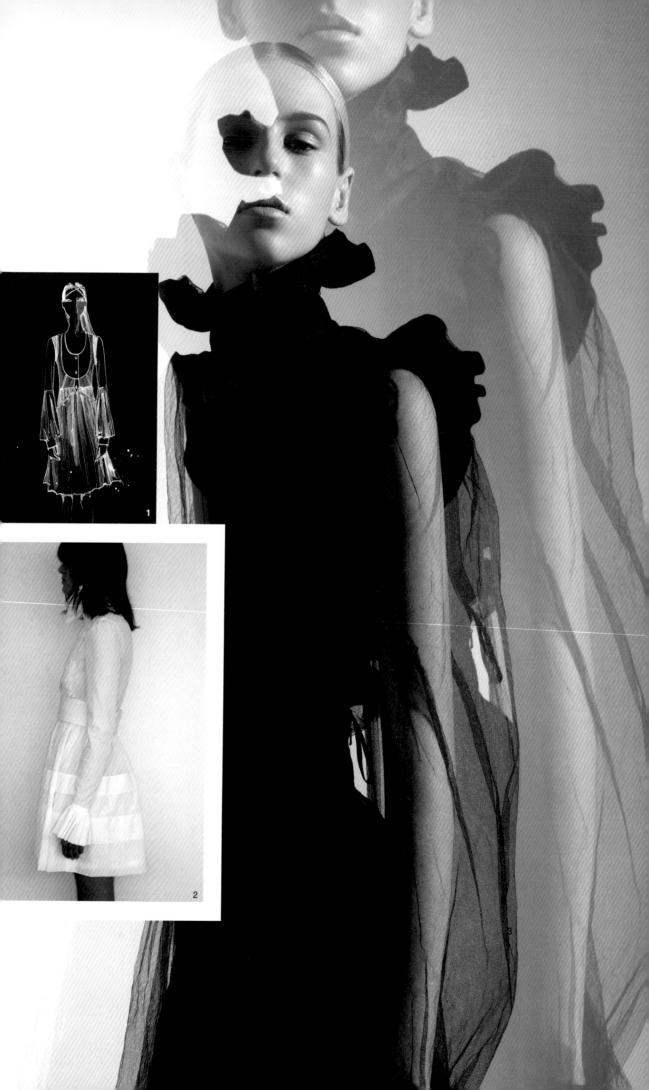

1

2

3

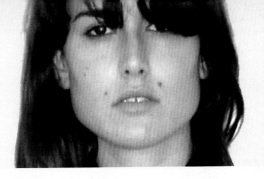

Danish-born Jens Laugesen studied haute-couture design at the Chambre Syndicale de la Couture Parisienne, graduating in 1991. He subsequently worked as a freelance fashion journalist for the Scandinavian press, before returning to Paris in 1994 to study for an MA in fashion management at the Institut Français de la Mode.

Jens Laugesen___51/100

In 2000 Laugesen moved to London to study at Central Saint Martins and graduated in 2002. Paris boutique Maria Luisa chose to exhibit his graduate collection in its store windows during Haute Couture Week in July 2002, and Laugesen's first runway presentation was held in the same year as part of Fashion East. In 2003 he was awarded the New Generation Award by the British Fashion Council, which allowed him to appear on the London Fashion Week official schedule.

How would you define your aesthetic? *My aesthetic is understated yet dramatic. I am very inspired by my Danish roots. Lately I have been informed by the work of Wilhelm Hammershøi, because I think his beautiful neoclassical interiors of nineteenth-century bourgeois apartments announce the modern abstract feel of Cubism. Like him, I portray architecture and a non-narrative mood in my collections.*

How would you describe your customer? *Someone who is very independent, who rejects not only the general fashion mood but also the commercial trends of the media and the high street. She is aiming to express her individual aesthetic and style.*

How would you describe your creative process? *My creative design process is ongoing. It is always about how you can morph different ideas or generic garments into new hybrids. From one season to another, you develop and you refine the process, and maybe after two or three years you finally achieve the technical execution you dreamt about initially.*

Who or what informs your work? *I am inspired by different things. It can be the way someone wears their own clothes, the way they make a personal statement. It can also be an old vintage research piece that inspires me to design a certain kind of garment again and again.*

www.jenslaugesen.com

1. Illustration for hybrid tuxedo/cocktail shirt dress, S/S 07. **2.** High-frill-collar shirt dress, S/S 07. **3.** High-frill tulle dress, Sophi Halette for Jens Laugesen, A/W 08. **4.** Satin and tulle dress and jacket, S/S 07. **5–8.** Cropped cape, knitted dress and Swarovski crystal leggings; neck-tie shirt with crinoline skirt; raw cut shirt with high-waist trousers; wool satin-front tea-dress with Swarovski crystal belt. ANDAM Award-winning A/W 07 collection. **9.** Cashmere cape coat, A/W 07. **10.** Mink cape, scarf and trench jacket by Kopenhagen Fur for Jens Laugesen, A/W 07. **11.** White tuxedo suit, A/W 06.

4

5

7

8

'*My aesthetic is understated yet dramatic*'——**Jens Laugesen**

9

10

11

1

2

4

5

Joel Diaz, the designer behind Jolibe, was born in The Dominican Republic. After learning dressmaking techniques from his mother, he attended Parsons the New School for Design in New York. He assisted Helmut Lang for almost five years, where his focus was on the development of innovative techniques as well as creating garments for celebrity clients.

Jolibe___*52/100*

Diaz went on to open a design consultancy studio, where projects have included working on the creation of the Autumn/Winter 06/07 Paco Rabanne collection, the Autumn and Spring 07 collections for Helmut Lang and ongoing work for Coach campaigns and Victoria's Secret shows. The studio has also collaborated with top stylists on editorials and worked on campaigns and celebrity wardrobes in the music and film industries. In 2007 Joel Diaz debuted *Jolibe* at Paris Fashion Week.

Defining his aesthetic as 'unpredictable' and his philosophy as being about 'participation', Diaz describes his customer as 'strong, confident and not afraid of risk'. He always starts a project without much direction, letting one step lead him to the next. As he explains, the process 'can go all over the place but editing is a key part of it. It's a question of going back and forth, an act of shuffling and building'.

For Diaz, contemporary fashion 'predicts a naïve or intellectual visual and tactile desire, and fulfils it'. Everything inspires the designer, who says that any ordinary thing can be translated into his work. His biggest challenge is to forget everything he knows 'to make room for newness'.

www.jolibe.com

1. Design sketch, S/S 08. **2.** Ruffled and darted organza and charmeuse dress, S/S 08. **3.** Silk-jersey t-shirt with wool trouser-skirt, A/W 07. **4.** Double-knit bolero, gabardine high-waisted trousers and poplin shirt, A/W 07. **5.** Technical-print silk-charmeuse and chiffon dress, S/S 08. **6.** Motor detail for cavalry twill coat, A/W 07.

1

Scottish print designer Jonathan Saunders graduated from Glasgow School of Art in 1999. He went on to Central Saint Martins and in 2002 obtained an MA in printed textiles. His graduate collection won him the Lancôme Colour Designs Award. In September 2006 he was awarded the Fashion Enterprise Award by the British Fashion Council.

Jonathan Saunders___*53/100*

Saunders coordinates designing his own label with consulting for some of the largest fashion houses in Europe. Using traditional silk-screening techniques, he has developed the concept of engineering prints around pattern pieces. In effect, each garment has its own specifically designed print rather that one standard print being used throughout a collection. Saunders uses up to twenty silk screens per design and has as many as twenty prints within one collection.

Describe your design philosophy. *My designs are based on the combination of process and technique.*

What is the most enjoyable part of design? *Research: exploring techniques and discovering images that inspire me, from fine art to design.*

How would you describe your customer? *It would be wrong to bracket the* Jonathan Saunders *customer into one particular demographic. Different pieces from each collection inspire different women. She has an appreciation of minimal elegance. She follows fashion, but is not led by it.*

How would you define contemporary fashion? *We live in a fast-moving and fast-changing environment. Fashion has to move with that. With our exposure to mass media, we absorb immeasurable amounts of information. In the first decade of the twenty-first century, I do not think we have a defined image such as in the 1960s, 1970s and 1980s. Instead, contemporary fashion is defined by how eclectic and diverse it is.*

Who or what informs your work? *I am inspired by any designer/artist/writer who has developed their creative identity over a period of time and has constantly evolved their craft, whether that fits into a current trend or not. I admire those who are receptive to the influence of the people and the environment that surrounds them.*

www.jonathan-saunders.com

1. Costume by Jonathan Saunders for 'Endangered Species', 2006. **2.** Cotton mac with detachable hood with long sleeved silk-knit dress, S/S 08. **3–6.** Yellow cashmere polo neck dress with degrade warp jacket and silk rope necklace; printed chiffon dress with black leather foil-printed belt and silk rope necklace; silk blouse and trousers in 'raining down' print with leather belt; cashmere polo neck dress layered with degrade chiffon dress and leather belt. All A/W 05. **7.** Long black, white and grey silk dress, A/W 06. **8.** Graphic-print dress, S/S 04.

2

'My designs are based on the combination of process and technique'
Jonathan Saunders

7

8

1

2

Polish-born Katarzyna Szczotarska moved to London in 1985 to study fashion design at Middlesex Polytechnic and London College of Fashion. She then worked for a number of internationally renowned design houses in England, Italy and France, and in 1997 she was employed by Martin Margiela, where she stayed for two years. In 2001 Szczotarska launched her own label and was awarded a Topshop New Generation designer award by the British Fashion Council, which she won again in 2003.

Katarzyna Szczotarska
——54/100

Szczotarska has developed a strong, modernist aesthetic using conceptual cutting and distinctive detailing. Her design style has been described as 'intellectual chic'. 'There are four key elements that I consider while designing: form, proportion, silhouette and the relation of the garment to the body. It is essential for me to have an idea and concept behind my design. These ideas drive design elements within the garment.'

For Szczotarska, references are derived from ideas: 'I am inspired by modern art and conceptual art. I also really like the classic age, old masters and the fifteenth-century lifestyle of the Italian and Spanish. I don't really get inspired by literal influences.' Within her distinct design aesthetic, Szczotarska has a clarity of ideas, which does not necessarily mean simplicity; rather a coherent interpretation of the concept as well as balanced detail. 'I dislike clutter unless it is an essential part of the intended concept,' she confirms.

www.katarzynaszczotarska.com

1. Silk shirt dress with oversized details, A/W 06. 2. Pearl-print cotton-jersey tunic, S/S 06. 3. Cotton tuck-top, S/S 05. 4. Mini houndstooth linen pencil skirt with self-stripe backless shirt, S/S 07. 5. Jersey polo shirt with oversized puff sleeves, S/S 05. 6–9. Viscose-cotton apron dress over silk-chiffon balloon-sleeve dress; Silk-satin sleeveless dress with back slash over silk balloon-sleeve top; drawstring-neck top with panel skirt; silk-satin dress with scarf neck. All A/W 07.

3

4

5

'There are four key elements that I consider while designing: form, proportion, silhouette and the relation of the garment to the body' __Katarzyna Szczotarska

7

8

9

Japanese-born Kanya Miki moved to San Diego in 1997 and studied fine art while teaching himself clothing design. He went on to study fashion at the Royal Academy of Fine Arts in Antwerp, Belgium, graduating in 2002 and becoming the first Japanese national ever to graduate from this prestigious university. After college Miki worked as an assistant designer for Walter Van Beirendonck and John Galliano before launching his own line, Kosmetique Label, in 2004. His first collection debuted in Paris in 2005.

Kosmetique Label___*55/100*

The philosophy behind *Kosmetique Label* is to create stylish unisex clothes – in the designer's own words, 'clothes with a new attitude' – and the design aesthetic is concerned with 'things that can feel, movement or sound'. The name of the label was chosen because Miki's aim is that his clothes enhance the figure in the same way that cosmetics enhance the face.

Based in Paris, Miki channels both his Japanese and European influences in to his designs, creating sophisticated clothing with an androgynous appeal, beautifully cut to produce an elegant silhouette. He extends his design aesthetic to both men and women by creating designs that only need to change in size to be suitable for different sexes.

Miki describes his customer as someone 'who likes a new spirit', and he finds that the most enjoyable part of designing clothes is when clients like what he has created. His intention is to make people look effortlessly refined, without being overtly formal, and he communicates this ideal through his stylish, sportswear-focused clothing.

www.kosmetiquelabel.com

1. Transformed tuxedo jacket and army pants, A/W 06. **2.** Army jacket with fox scarf, A/W 06. **3.** Location shoot, A/W 07. **4–7.** Faux-fur blouson with cotton t-shirt and cashmere-mix trousers; cashmere-mix P-coat, satin-hemmed wool jacket and asymmetric army pants; wool army jacket with synthetic tight pants; cashmere-mix jacket with cotton shirt. All A/W 06. **8–9.** Lambskin leather long coat with wide pants and synthetic v-neck, A/W 07.

'Clothes with a new attitude'
Kosmetique Label

9

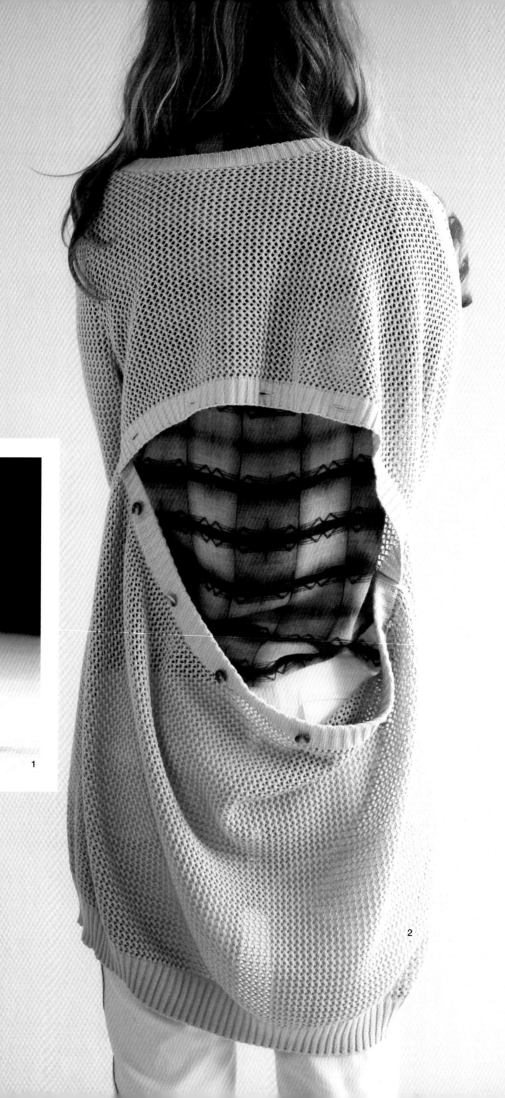

1

2

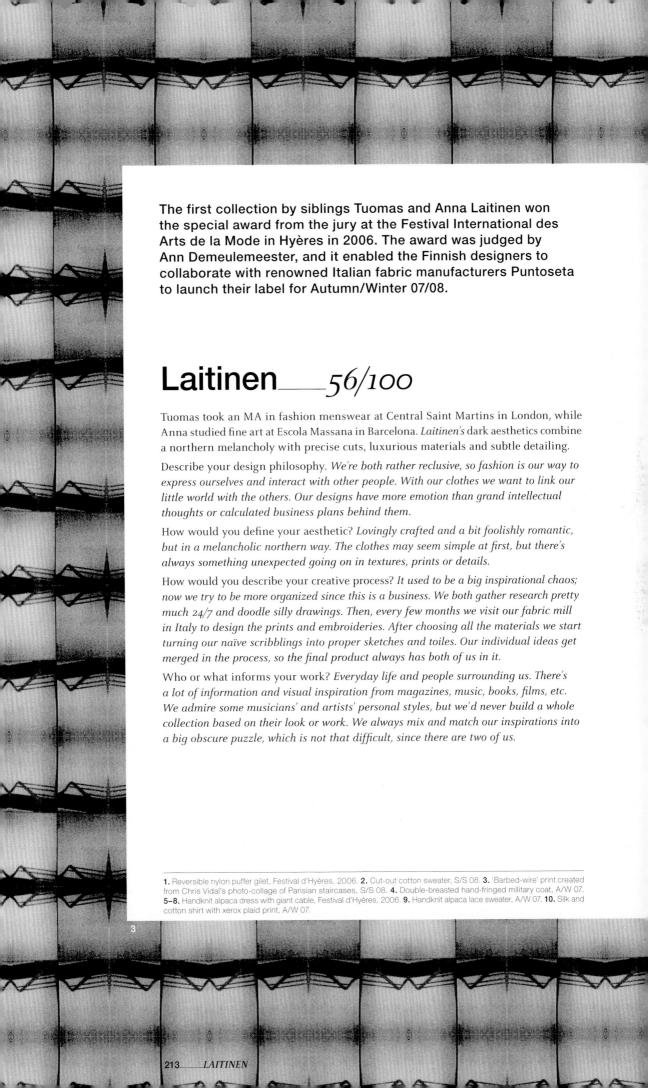

The first collection by siblings Tuomas and Anna Laitinen won the special award from the jury at the Festival International des Arts de la Mode in Hyères in 2006. The award was judged by Ann Demeulemeester, and it enabled the Finnish designers to collaborate with renowned Italian fabric manufacturers Puntoseta to launch their label for Autumn/Winter 07/08.

Laitinen___*56/100*

Tuomas took an MA in fashion menswear at Central Saint Martins in London, while Anna studied fine art at Escola Massana in Barcelona. *Laitinen's* dark aesthetics combine a northern melancholy with precise cuts, luxurious materials and subtle detailing.

Describe your design philosophy. *We're both rather reclusive, so fashion is our way to express ourselves and interact with other people. With our clothes we want to link our little world with the others. Our designs have more emotion than grand intellectual thoughts or calculated business plans behind them.*

How would you define your aesthetic? *Lovingly crafted and a bit foolishly romantic, but in a melancholic northern way. The clothes may seem simple at first, but there's always something unexpected going on in textures, prints or details.*

How would you describe your creative process? *It used to be a big inspirational chaos; now we try to be more organized since this is a business. We both gather research pretty much 24/7 and doodle silly drawings. Then, every few months we visit our fabric mill in Italy to design the prints and embroideries. After choosing all the materials we start turning our naïve scribblings into proper sketches and toiles. Our individual ideas get merged in the process, so the final product always has both of us in it.*

Who or what informs your work? *Everyday life and people surrounding us. There's a lot of information and visual inspiration from magazines, music, books, films, etc. We admire some musicians' and artists' personal styles, but we'd never build a whole collection based on their look or work. We always mix and match our inspirations into a big obscure puzzle, which is not that difficult, since there are two of us.*

---

1. Reversible nylon puffer gilet, Festival d'Hyères, 2006. **2.** Cut-out cotton sweater, S/S 08. **3.** 'Barbed-wire' print created from Chris Vidal's photo-collage of Parisian staircases, S/S 08. **4.** Double-breasted hand-fringed military coat, A/W 07. **5–8.** Handknit alpaca dress with giant cable, Festival d'Hyères, 2006. **9.** Handknit alpaca lace sweater, A/W 07. **10.** Silk and cotton shirt with xerox plaid print, A/W 07.

5

6

4

7

8

'Lovingly crafted and a bit foolishly romantic, but in a melancholic Northern way' **___Laitinen**

9

10

1

2

'I make clothes for whoever relates to them; if it makes them feel better about themselves then my existence has a real purpose,' explains Portuguese fashion designer Louis de Gama, who has been living in London since 1992. After studying garment technology, de Gama studied for a fashion design degree at the University of Westminster in London where he worked with designer Tristan Webber.

Louis de Gama___*57/100*

The label *Louis de Gama* was established in 2000 with the launch of the first collection at London Fashion Week. The acclaimed shop Browns Focus in London bought the entire collection.

de Gama's collections are defined as being 'feminine with an edge' and wearable. The label is known for the designer's distinct use of different materials, for example, his mix of leather with silk chiffons. Life's vicissitudes, struggles, people's attitudes and behaviours, books and music all inspire de Gama.

For de Gama, the most enjoyable part of the design process is the interaction with his assistants. 'The making process in the studio is definitely the most rewarding. Fashion shows are primarily to please a hungry, obsessed and insecure audience and sometimes true admirers. It is spontaneous and unpredictable. We often rely on mistakes to progress.'

Believing his customers have strong personalities, de Gama is eager to please them: 'They use the clothes as extensions of themselves and as tools of communication.' He sees contemporary fashion as a huge media business. 'As long as you get the press and use it well, you are bound to succeed. There will always be some poor soul willing to buy your product, irrespectively.'

To retain his modernity, de Gama does not conform to nor follow contemporary culture. 'Being inquisitive, a little cynical and keeping my innate, raw energy is vital,' he explains.

www.louisdegama.com

1. Wrap-front top with matching bikini briefs and bag, S/S 05. **2.** Tie-front dress, S/S 06 Lookbook. **3.** Inspiration wall in the studio. **4–7.** Fringed skirt and top with fringed collar; leather waistcoat with flamenco-style skirt; embellished leather top with fringed skirt; leather and chiffon patchwork dress. All A/W 05. **8–9.** Chiffon and sequin dresses, A/W 04.

3

LOUIS DE GAMA

4

5

6

7

'We often rely on mistakes to progress'___**Louis de Gama**

8

9

1

2

'I do not have a specific philosophy as such,' explains Danish fashion designer Louise Amstrup. 'However, I think it's very important that fashion is there to emphasize and flatter the individual, not to overshadow the person, but to complement her.'

Louise Amstrup___*58/100*

Amstrup grew up in Germany and later returned to Düsseldorf to complete her studies. In 2003 she graduated from the Akademie Mode Design, where she was awarded the Graduate Talent prize. After college, Amstrup worked with such influential designers as Alexander McQueen, Jonathan Saunders, Sophia Kokosalaki, Alistair Carr and Catherine Walker.

'I love designing looks that are contemporary and promote individuality,' enthuses Amstrup, whose designs are powerful yet feminine, with a soul to suit the female shape. 'You will see a hint of the strict and constructed meets the soft and surreal, but always with slightly ironic stitching. Somehow my collections always end up being very eclectic.'

Key to Amstrup's style is an attention to detail and fine tailoring skills teamed with the use of luxurious fabrics. She enjoys the research process: 'A phase where you let your guard down and let yourself drown in such inspiration as moods, music, art, etc. I also love the final bits where everything comes together, and the collection comes alive.'

'For me contemporary fashion consists of many elements that make a whole: reflections of the past, glimpses of the future and a final individual and creative touch that makes it unique and present.' Amstrup finds it difficult to define her customers but believes that they are creative and imaginative women whom she admires and enjoys seeing interpreting her clothes to fit their personality. Amstrup's appeal lies in her ability to fuse precisely tailored elements with beautifully draped garments resulting in inherently contemporary ideas.

www.louise-amstrup.com

1. Belted black dress, A/W 06. **2.** Cotton striped blouse, black zip pencil skirt and customized zip hat, S/S 08. **3.** Photoshoot, S/S 08. **4.** Cotton trench with yellow draped silk skirt, S/S 07. **5.** Black trapeze skirt with customized vest top, S/S 07. **6.** Draped light-grey coat, S/S 07.

3

'*Somehow my collections always end up being very eclectic*'
Louise Amstrup

4

5

6

1

2

3

Lutz Huelle and David Ballu comprise Lutz. After studying at Central Saint Martins, Huelle worked with Martin Margiela for three years, where he was responsible for the knitwear and artisan lines. Ballu worked for thirteen years for Cosmopolitan Cosmetics, which makes perfumes for Gucci, Dunhill and Mountblanc. Since 2002 the Lutz label has been a member of the Fédération Française de la Couture du Prêt-à-Porter des Couturiers et des Créateurs de Mode. In 2000 Lutz was awarded the ANDAM (Association Nationale pour le Développement des Arts de la Mode) prize, which included a bursary from Yves Saint Laurent Couture, and the label won it again in 2002 with a bursary from Henri Bendel New York.

Lutz——59/100

Lutz describe their design philosophy as 'decontextualization' – taking things out of context, mixing and matching styles and genres, cutting and pasting elements. 'I like things that seem fairly familiar at first, but are not really when looked at closely', Huelle explains.

Starting a collection is always enjoyable for Huelle. 'It's like leaving the office on a Friday night, knowing that the whole weekend is in front of you, and anything could happen. It's only later that things become more complicated, when fabrics turn up late or prototypes don't work out.'

Treating every collection as if it were his first, Huelle feels he has to prove himself over and over again. 'It's a work in progress, in the sense that I constantly look around me to see what and how people wear clothes, and I keep a diary of ideas that I go through every time I start a new collection.'

People around him, friends, popular culture, films, travelling and especially music inspire Huelle. 'My work is about the life I lead at this moment, not about somebody else's life fifty years ago.' Huelle believes that wearing his clothes is not so much a question of age or body shape, but more about an attitude or an alternative. 'The most important thing is to make people feel good about themselves, both physically and mentally.'

1. Silk sports vest and high-waisted skirt, A/W 03. **2.** Belted mohair jacket with leather buttons and viscose skirt, A/W 07. **3.** Deconstructed jacket with button-through dress. **4.** Lurex knit with cotton skirt. **5.** Catwalk show A/W 06. **6.** Fringed wool jacket, A/W 04. **7–8.** MO-DE Exhibition in Tokyo. **9.** Peacoat dress worn with 'rose' earrings, A/W 03.

7

LUTZ

'I like things that seem fairly familiar at first, but are not really when looked at closely' ___**Lutz**

8 LUTZ

9

Indian designer Manish Arora made his debut at London Fashion Week in 2005. Having already received substantial creative recognition in India, he brought his distinct aesthetic to the West. His collections are always an exuberant mix of colour and texture, with rich fabrics often beaded, printed or embroidered. His Indian heritage is a great influence on his work.

Manish Arora___*60/100*

In 1995 Arora graduated from the National Institute of Fashion Technology in New Delhi and set up his own label in 1997. In 2000 he represented India at Hong Kong Fashion Week and participated at the first ever India Fashion Week held in New Delhi. In the same year he also launched his second label, *Fish Fry*, showing the collection in six leading cities in India. In 2002 the first flagship store for *Fish Fry* was opened in New Delhi, and the second store opened a year later in India's commercial capital of Mumbai.

Arora's designs began to attract the attention of international buyers, and Maria Luisa bought his Spring/Summer 04 collection for her prestigious Parisian store. He started an export business, retailing at eight stores in Europe, and in 2004 won a prize for the best ready-to-wear collection at the Indian Fashion Awards.

Describe your design philosophy. *Listening to my creative instincts without caring much about the consequences.*

How would you define your aesthetic? *My creative aesthetic is unusually interesting, loud and innovative.*

What is the most enjoyable part of design? *The story or the concept behind the design is what is most interesting.*

How would you describe your customer? *My customer is one who experiments, likes colour and doesn't go for anything ordinary.*

How would you describe your creative process? *I take inspiration from everyday life. I decide upon a theme and start my research, then develop an interpretation of the theme. I listen to my creative instincts and follow them while designing.*

How would you define contemporary fashion? *Contemporary fashion can be defined as being innovative but wearable.*

What is the most challenging aspect of design? *Believing in your idea: having confidence until the completion of any design.*

www.manisharora.ws

1. Sequined dress, hat by Louis Mariette, S/S 07. 2. Garment print, S/S 08. 3–6. Silk and net underlay skirt; silk hand-embroidered jacket; silk dress; silk kimono top and skirt. S/S 06. 7. Skirts and sweaters encrusted with hand-embroidered motifs from Eastern and Western traditions, A/W 06.

2

'My creative aesthetic is unusually interesting, loud and innovative.'
___**Manish Arora**

1

2

3

UK-based fashion designers Benjamin Kirchhoff and Edward Meadham launched their menswear label in 2002 after graduating from Central Saint Martins in London. In 2006 the design duo introduced a focused range of womenswear that had its own identity while retaining all of the elements that helped to create their distinctive menswear aesthetic.

Meadham/Kirchhoff___*61/100*

In September 2005 an expert panel chose *Meadham/Kirchhoff* from a list of thirty designers to take part in Fashion East MAN, a joint event between Fashion East and Topman, to promote London's menswear talent. This was the first show in London for eight years dedicated exclusively to menswear.

In their menswear line, Meadham and Kirchhoff explore ideals of masculinity. Questioning notions of masculinity and ideas of masculine proportions, they look at ways of redefining the male body without making it look awkward. 'We have never really been about boyishness but we've never been "grown-up" either', they explain. 'We are very much about balance and we tend to use the same fabrics for a few seasons; we have trademarks that we have used since the beginning.'

Research is the most enjoyable part of the design process for Meadham and Kirchhoff They cite films as their main source of inspiration: 'In between collections we tend to watch a lot of movies from a specific genre, and elements from them influence us and inform the mood and style of the collection.' Cinecittà film-studio productions, 1940s film noir, Jean Cocteau's and Jean Genet's films have all informed various collections.

The most demanding aspect of design for the team is to constantly create something new and to communicate their ideas and concept into a garment. 'We don't use a lot of clothing references when we design and we work with a mood so our message has to be understood somehow once the garment is realized.'

The *Meadham/Kirchhoff* label is distinct in contemporary fashion as it straddles both menswear and womenswear, successfully producing modern clothing that challenges and pushes fashion forward.

www.meadhamkirchhoff.com

1. Tartan shirt with embroidered lace collar, A/W 07. **2.** Draped shirt, A/W 05. **3.** Cotton and lace shirt and lurex skirt, S/S 08. **4.** Research wall, menswear, S/S 07. **5.** Cut-away dress, A/W 07. **6.** Collage from S/S 04 Lookbook. **7.** Quilted jacket, A/W 07. **8.** Jacket with zip detail, S/S 08.

4

5

6

'We have never really been about boyishness but we've never been "grown-up" either' __Meadham/Kirchhoff

8

7

1

2

Born and raised in Japan, Miki Fukai graduated with an MA in fashion from Central Saint Martins in 2002. Previously she had worked as a fashion stylist, costume designer and womenswear designer in both London and Tokyo. Fukai launched her own womenswear label in 2003, and in 2006 she was awarded her third New Generation sponsorship at London Fashion Week. In 2007 she introduced a men's line called Man Miki Fukai.

Miki Fukai___62/100

Describe your design philosophy. *I very much like simple classic clothing that has a strong focus on detail. For example, I love exploring ways of making even a classic sweatshirt exceptional in some way. I am about jeans, t-shirts and sweatshirts. I am also interested in creating showpieces that have huge amounts of handwork. Although this is contrary to the whole jeans and t-shirts idea, the garments generally have the same feeling due to the materials I work with.*

How would you define your aesthetic? *My aesthetic is bound in the casual. What is relevant for me is what I see people wear on a day-to-day basis.*

What is the most enjoyable part of design? *Research is often most enjoyable as I can step out of the boundaries of fashion in real terms.*

How would you describe your creative process? *Once I have completed all my research, I make boards in the studio and edit the visual references into stories. The references then become abstract over a period of time and experimentation. I also work closely with my stylist Jodie Barnes and right-hand-man Aki. We discuss the evolution of the ideas and, by the end, out pops the collection.*

How would you define contemporary fashion? *Contemporary fashion has one foot firmly placed in the past and the other in the future.*

What is the most challenging aspect of design? *Drawing. I am terrible.*

How are you personally innovative in fashion design? *I like to find new ways of working with material and detailing to create something that feels modern and relevant.*

www.mikifukai.com

1. Patchwork vintage-denim jacket and jeans, A/W 05. 2. Patchwork vintage-denim military jacket, A/W 06. 3. Shirt and corduroy skirt, A/W 05. 4. Metric organza jacket and patchwork vintage-denim hotpants, S/S 07. 5. Patchwork vintage-denim corset dress, S/S 06. 6. Nylon utility jacket, A/W 05. 7. Lurex-silk balloon dress, A/W 06. 8. Chunky mohair plaited and knitted silk-wool jersey, A/W 05.

3

4

5

6

'I love exploring ways of making even a classic sweatshirt exceptional in some way'___Miki Fukai

1

2

3

Japanese-born Mikio Sakabe studied at ESMOD (Ecole de Mode Internationale) in Paris and then attended the Hogeschool in Antwerp, graduating in 2006. Sakabe's final-year collection explored 'opposites' within a framework of men's basics. His starting point was Manga and how two-dimensional drawing can be communicated onto fabric through printing. His garments were constructed like three-dimensional buildings, creating mini cities that morphed from his clothes.

Mikio Sakabe___63/100

Sakabe was awarded the Special Jury Prize at ITS#5 in Trieste, Italy, and also won an award given by the Flemish government for enterprise and innovation. In 2006 he exhibited his work at Walter van Beirendonck's 'Walter' store in Belgium. A project with the International Flavors and Fragrance (IFF), working with Louis Vuitton in 2004 and collaborating with Veronique Branquinho on a magazine have all raised Sakabe's profile on the international fashion scene.

For Sakabe, the most important thing is balance, which gives his work life. He loves the idea of being able to talk to people through his designs and is inspired by the underground culture 'that nobody can stop'. When asked to describe his creative process, Sakabe says, 'I try to forget my common sense and touch my unconscious'. For him, expressing new emotions is the most challenging aspect of design. Sakabe has become well known for fusing Japanese quirkiness with an acute appreciation of cutting technique and technical skills for customers he describes as 'super unisex'.

www.mikiosakabe.com

1. Bow-front dress, 'Industrial Dolls', S/S 08. 2. Jumpsuit and printed cape, graduate collection, A/W 06. 3. Grey jacket with wide trousers, A/W 06. 4. Graphic print ideas, A/W 06. 5. Padded garment, highschool 'Bed' collection, 2005. 6. Printed shirt and tie, A/W 06. 7. Padded skirt, 2005. 8. Pastel tracksuit, 'Industrial Dolls', S/S 08.

5

6

'I try to forget my common sense and touch my unconscious'
___**Mikio Sakabe**

7

8

1

3

4

While consulting for the Italian label Max Mara, Sierra Leonean Abdul Koroma and UK-born Andrew Jones met, both having graduated from London's Kingston School of Fashion but in different years. Together they formed Modernist in 2005 as an entry to Fashion Fringe, an annual competition held during London Fashion Week.

Modernist___*64/100*

Modernist provides an alternative take on luxury and femininity, with a streamlined, refined and forward-looking aesthetic. Each collection features a desirable mix of luxurious fabrics styled in a casual way and immaculately finished. The silhouette draws attention to the unusual use of fabric and the inventive detailing.

How would you define your aesthetic? *Our look is quite streamlined and graphic but there is also a more playful side. It's about taking mundane, ordinary things and lifting them out of context, elevating them into luxury products. We're obsessed by finishes and unexpected use of fabrics: a biker jacket made out of industrial paper and lined in black washed satin; a soft cashmere coat fabric used for a bra. So much fashion these days is about the instantly recognizable. It's tempting, but we prefer working from the sidelines – there is no grand, theatrical statement.*

How would you describe your customer? *From late twenties upward, confident, not a slave to trends. We want to make women feel special, unique, feminine and sexy without looking vulgar. Our customer enjoys fashion and is self-aware. And she always wears heels!*

How would you define contemporary fashion? *The Internet has changed everything. The world's smaller, but it also makes it harder to get your message across when everyone's vying for space and attention. It's all about now, now, now, me, me, me and new, new, new. This idea of the quick fix.*

Who or what informs your work? *AK: Music, people on the street, bad photographs and 1950s art like Manzoni, Fontana and Rothko. AJ: In a word, contrast. The mixing of opposites – luxe and poor, raw and refined, techno and organic. Also, the use and deliberate misuse of craftsmanship and the effect that digital technology is having on fashion and on life in general.*

www.modernistonline.com

1–4. Silk-satin rose-print t-shirt with satin skirt; silk cropped jacket and skirt with leather bra top; leather jacket with pleated sleeves and double-layered jersey dress; cotton shift dress with silk-taffeta biker jacket. 'Evolution of the Modern Rose', S/S 07. **5.** Research wall for S/S 06 'Domestic Bliss' collection.

5

1

2

Originally trained as a hairdresser at Vidal Sassoon, London-born Nasir Mazhar is at the forefront of conceptual hat design. After becoming creatively frustrated with hairdressing, Mazhar had the urge to create for himself and to move away from commercial hair-salon work. He undertook an evening class in hat making and worked with theatrical hat maker Mark Wheeler, where he learned the technical and creative skills that fuel his current practice.

Nasir Mazhar___*65/100*

Although his three-dimensional creations have little resemblance to headgear, they are made to be worn on and around the head. With inspirations as diverse as Grace Jones, Greek peasants and microphones, Mazhar's ideas are inherently bold and dynamic. Using such materials as leather, wire and mesh, Mazhar presents one-off pieces that are conceptual yet possess a sense of humour and extreme modernity.

How would you define your aesthetic? *There is no way to define it. It switches from comical childish fun to dark bold aggressiveness to historical classics.*

What is the most enjoyable part of design? *The thought that this could be reality soon.*

How would you describe your customer? *At the moment there isn't a particular type I have in mind.*

How would you describe your creative process? *There isn't one. No method, no guidelines. Sometimes it starts with a design, sometimes an idea, an image, a scene, an object. I let myself be free and let what happens happen.*

How would you define contemporary fashion? *No comment.*

Who or what informs your work? *Everything and anything.*

How are you personally innovative in fashion design? *By using everything and anything as inspiration. I live in a very mixed-up city in many ways, which is extremely modern on its own. Giving yourself freedom and being open and accepting. There should be few barriers in what we do.*

1. Ostrich hood on dressmaker's dummy, S/S 08. **2.** Cereal mask. **3.** Miscellaneous materials in the studio during preparations for the S/S 08 collection.

3

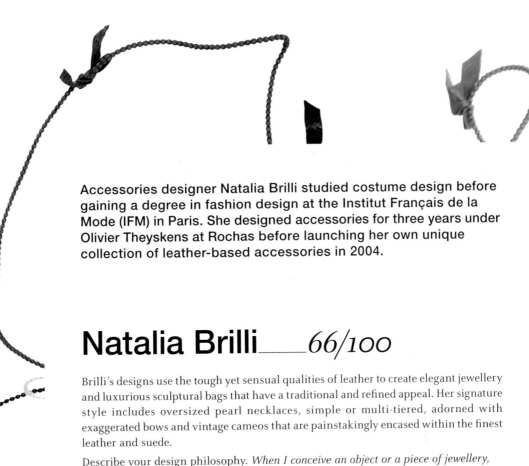

Accessories designer Natalia Brilli studied costume design before gaining a degree in fashion design at the Institut Français de la Mode (IFM) in Paris. She designed accessories for three years under Olivier Theyskens at Rochas before launching her own unique collection of leather-based accessories in 2004.

Natalia Brilli___*66/100*

Brilli's designs use the tough yet sensual qualities of leather to create elegant jewellery and luxurious sculptural bags that have a traditional and refined appeal. Her signature style includes oversized pearl necklaces, simple or multi-tiered, adorned with exaggerated bows and vintage cameos that are painstakingly encased within the finest leather and suede.

Describe your design philosophy. *When I conceive an object or a piece of jewellery, I try not to render the appearance of reality but to express a hidden meaning. With the sheathing technique [a popular Art Deco method of covering items in a cocoon of leather], I appropriate the typical codes of classic jewellery but I only leave an imprint effect of the pieces – monochrome, but lighter, more graphic, their essence freed of what is unnecessary.*

How would you define your aesthetic? *It's the mix of two cultures, me being Italian-Belgian: the dark and ghostly heritage from the north combined with a cultivated aesthetic elegance from the south.*

What is the most enjoyable part of design? *Research and the evolution of the creative process. From the beginning to the final result when the object takes shape in your hands. It's a magical moment, but one that can sometimes turn into tragedy!*

How would you describe your customer? *There is no typical profile. Some buy my jewellery to wear as fashion accessories; others like to collect pieces like fetishes that they put on show on their furniture or in a display window.*

Who or what informs your work? *Women such as Edith Sitwell, Nancy Cunard or Charlotte Rampling for their out-of-time beauty and their typically British spirit, their blurry, ghostly aura, the mystery surrounding them.*

What is the most challenging aspect of design? *The paradox of creating something that is new and yet resists the influence of time.*

www.nataliabrilli.fr

1. Handmade leather headpiece, S/S 07. **2.** Lambskin leather covered pearl necklaces. **3–4.** Handmade customized lambskin leather Vespa helmets. **5.** Lambskin leather covered necklaces and ruched leather gloves with elbow detail.

2

'When I conceive an object or a piece of jewellery, I try not to render the appearance of reality but to express a hidden meaning'——**Natalia Brilli**

3

4

London-born Nathan Jenden studied at Central Saint Martins and then at the Royal College of Art. On graduating, he spent a year as a designer at Kenzo before going to work with John Galliano in Paris. In 1998 Jenden moved to New York as design director for Daryl K's men's and women's collections. He joined Diane von Furstenberg as creative director in 2001, where he expands her line of iconic designs as well as building the brand.

Nathan Jenden___*67/100*

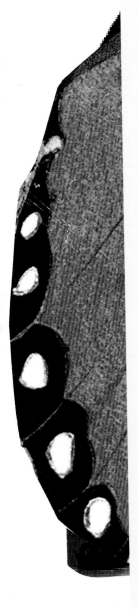

In 2006 Jenden launched his own label with a runway show at Lady Mendl's Tea Salon during New York Fashion Week. 'Angel Heart' was his first collection, followed by 'The Collector' for Spring/Summer 07. Jenden's ambition is to present collections that fill the gap between the artisan and the factory by using craftspeople to hand finish garments that are durable, lasting and of a beautiful quality.

Describe your design philosophy. *Don't take yourself too seriously.*

How would you define your aesthetic? *Random but refined.*

What is the most enjoyable part of design? *Draping on the stand.*

How would you describe your customer? *Strong, tongue-in-cheek, feminine.*

How would you describe your creative process? *Refining the random.*

How would you define contemporary fashion? *A bit tame.*

Who or what informs your work? *People of character. They can be from anywhere, everywhere and of any age, but people of character always teach you something.*

What is the most challenging aspect of design? *Having things executed beautifully. There is a very technical process, which is more like engineering, that edifies the creative process. Without this, clothes can look cheap and shoddy.*

How are you personally innovative in fashion design? *I don't necessarily seek to be innovative. With both the* Nathan Jenden *and the* DVF *lines I see so many clothes that I know what looks fresh and what doesn't. Being 'fresh' is more important than being innovative.*

www.nathanjenden.com

1–4. Cotton linen blazer, skirt with patchwork pleating and three-tiered sunburst silk-organza petticoat; coated cotton oversized parka with three-tiered silk-organza petticoat; silk-organza twill and satin-faced organza with silk-jersey cocktail dress; viscose poet blouse with cotton-linen awning-stripe knicker short. All S/S 08. 5. Inspirational image from Nathan Jenden's sketchbook.

5

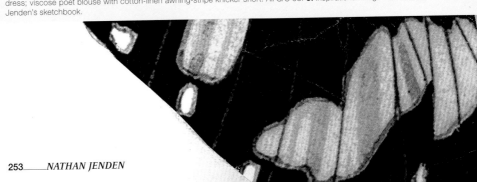

1

2

After studying art and design in Edinburgh, Niki Taylor gained a place at the Scottish College of Textiles at Heriot Watt University, where she learned cutting and tailoring skills. On graduating she established the label Olanic – the name being an anagram of her full first name, Nicola. Taylor debuted her first mainline collection at Rendez-Vous, Paris, in October 2004 and has exhibited subsequent collections at London Fashion Week.

Olanic___68/100

Drawing influence from underground pop culture, art, music and film, the *Olanic* label is driven by the idea of investing everyday, practical styles with a quirky, tailored edge. Taylor's vision was that *Olanic* would not exist in the fashion world alone. Dedicated to the idea of cross-collaboration, she works with film-maker and video director Sandy Hutton to create short films that are based around *Olanic* designs.

British newspaper *The Times* tipped *Olanic* as being one of the 'Top Ten Fashion Names to Watch', and Taylor was runner-up in the Scottish Creative Entrepreneur awards and shortlisted for the Scottish Designer of the Year in 2005 and 2006.

Describe your design philosophy. *Design is about experimenting, pushing new ideas and boundaries and having fun with it!*

How would you define your aesthetic? *Heightening everyday garments and objects with an individual flair. It is a playful aesthetic.*

What is the most enjoyable part of design? *Research and being inspired.*

How would you describe your customer? *Effortlessly stylish with individuality.*

How would you describe your creative process? *Enjoyable and creative in all areas.*

How would you define contemporary fashion? *Eclectic.*

Who or what informs your work? *Mainly underground music and art.*

What is the most challenging aspect of design? *Money.*

How are you personally innovative in fashion design? *I don't try too hard and always look forward.*

www.olanic.co.uk

1. Cotton jersey shift dress with hand-cut leather yoke, S/S 08. 2. Plaid skirt with check swing coat and jersey hooded bodysuit, A/W 06. 3. Distorted angles print by Niki Taylor, S/S 07. 4. Designer's studio. 5. Jersey and mesh t-shirt with layered leather skirt, A/W 07. 6. Digital stripe dress, S/S 06. 7. Patch jersey dress, S/S 08.

3

*...n is about experimenting,
...g new ideas and boundaries
and having fun with it!'* ___**Olanic**

6

7

1

2

A Cambridge graduate and former city banker, Osman Yousefzada retrained at Central Saint Martins to pursue his creative ambitions. He graduated in 2003 and went on to show his collections at London Fashion Week.

Osman Yousefzada___*69/100*

'My work revolves around ideas of ethnicity, costume. These are fused together to create new shapes and silhouettes,' explains Yousefzada. 'I am interested in this fusion, much like how new immigrants tend to adopt different dress, or fuse different dress styles when they go to a host country.' Yousefzada embeds these ideas in his designs through strong tailoring and distinctive drapery. The ethos of the clothes is to present a sculpted body, and Yousefzada describes his aesthetic as 'Tribal Bauhaus'. He strips away the excess in his clothes and streamlines them to make the body as defined and powerful as possible. The backs of his designs are never neglected and have inbuilt drama. He likens the end result to being architectural, like looking at a building from different angles.

The most enjoyable part of design for Yousefzada is the initial development process: 'This is the part that does not seem like work, nor a chore, but it just comes naturally. I am always searching for new ideas and what is quite interesting, even when I go back to the same source, is that you always see something new.' He cites books, paintings and people on the street as key inspirations. From there initial ideas are formed and sketched, and then further developed into three-dimensional shapes.

Not driven by attempts to be modern, Yousefzada aims to be relevant in his approach to what women want to wear. 'I think fashion is very much about the disposable at present, and there is a lesser emphasis on something that will last. We are looking for instant gratification.'

The conflict between tradition and modernity in Yousefzada's clothes creates an interesting paradox. His clothes are precise, well tailored and finished with soft draping that creates simple yet directional pieces.

www.osmanyousefzada.com

1. White leather one-button blouson. 2. Metal bodices, 'Tribal Bauhaus', S/S 08. 3. Skirt with metallic detail, 'Icon', A/W 07. 4. Illustration by Yousefzada. 5. Leather zip-jacket with frill, A/W 07. 6–9. Fitted jersey with draped tulip-shaped skirt; funnel-neck coat; cream wool shift with panel of human hair; sculpted jacket. All 'Pilgrim', A/W 06.

4

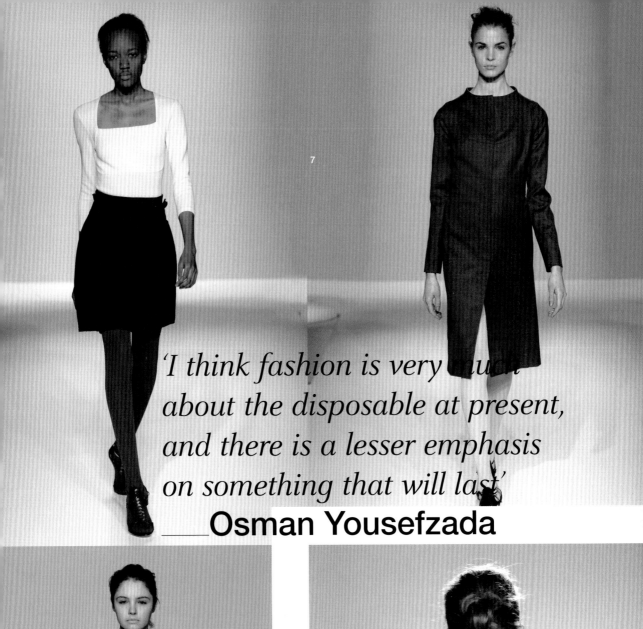

7

'I think fashion is very much about the disposable at present, and there is a lesser emphasis on something that will last'
___**Osman Yousefzada**

8

9

1

2

After studying at the Stockholm Cutting Academy in Sweden where he specialized in the construction of menswear, Patrik Söderstam graduated from Central Saint Martins in London in 2003. He has worked for contemporary British designer Robert Cary-Williams and also as a costume designer and stylist for Nokia, Nike and Absolut Vodka.

Patrik Söderstam___70/100

Describe your design philosophy. *I design with myself in mind. My design ideas circle around my life, what I need and how I want to express myself. I am interested in pushing boundaries and wearing things that are out of the norm. I am not into theatrical things or expression. I am into real everyday life stuff, my style.*

What is the most enjoyable part of design? *I enjoy working in the studio by myself, experimenting with new shapes. I like the process of making new patterns to make up test garment after test garment. I also enjoy making the presentations, the photographs, the graphics, the film. I don't like doing the traditional catwalk with models – I hate that. I will probably need to do catwalks again at some point – but it is all so boring. I am into progressive stuff.*

How would you describe your customer? *People who I feel fit my designs are free open-minded thinkers. They are arty rebels who know what they are about.*

How would you describe your creative process? *I work on the same project all the time: a collection of garments I need for my life. I would like to get it done so I can move on with other projects – maybe for someone other than myself. I am not very happy with what I have come up with so far, so I will continue experimenting until I have a wardrobe that I feel I can live in.*

How would you define successful menswear? *Successful menswear for me is something that allows a man to express himself in the same way as a woman can do but in a masculine way. Something that shows your own persona, not just an attitude.*

www.patriksoderstam.com

1. Exhibition in Stockholm store. **2.** Oversized denim jacket and jeans with padded shoulders and calves, 'The Sod', S/S 06. **3.** T-shirt print. **4–7.** Baggy-crotch trousers in stretch denim; reversible hooded jacket; baggy printed nylon trousers with metallic-silver panels; vest with baggy printed trousers. All 'Orgasm', A/W 03. **8.** White cotton shirt and tight stretch-denim trousers with padded calves, white panels and lycra pockets, S/S 06. **9.** Unisex garments, 'TV', A/W 04.

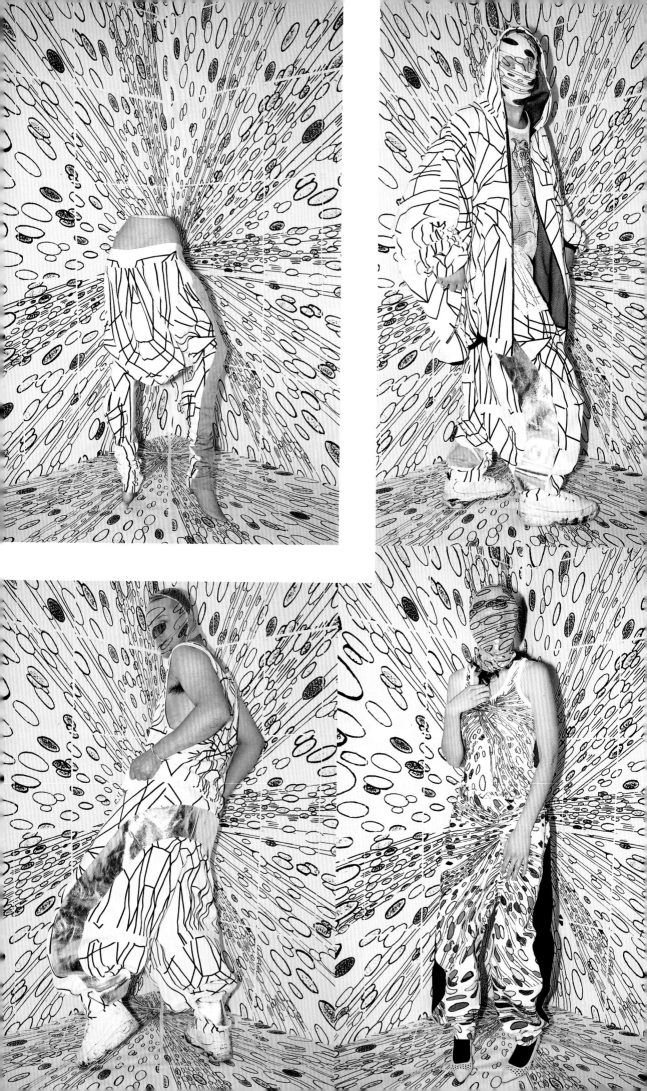

'*I work on the same project all the time: a collection of garments I need for my life*'
Patrik Söderstam

8

9

Artist and designer Carolin Lerch was born in Austria and moved to Belgium in 1995 to study fashion at the Royal Academy of Fine Arts in Antwerp. She set up Pelican Avenue in 2004, based on a 'de-celerated' aesthetic that questions the conventional codes of fashion and opposes the constantly changing trends of the Western fashion industry.

Pelican Avenue___71/100

On graduating from the Royal Academy of Fine Arts in 1999, Lerch was invited to show her student collection to the international press at the French Festival International des Arts de la Mode in Hyères. Following this, she assisted the Paris-based fashion designer Patrick van Ommeslaeghe and then worked for two years as a production manager for Bernhard Willhelm in Antwerp while studying mixed media, again at the Royal Academy.

Developing her own video and art projects in Belgium and Germany, Lerch co-curated 'Aller-retour', an exhibition about young Flemish fashion design and fine art in Nantes, France. In 2004 she founded *Pelican Avenue*, a fashion label that represents her own designs but also functions as a collaborative base for artists from different disciplines.

Lerch's designs are influenced by personal and formal reflections, channelled in to functional, wearable clothes that are often created from simple geometric forms. She shuns continuous production by producing limited editions of her designs, and presents her collections through a range of media, from photography and video to installation and performance.

It is important to Lerch to question the label after every project in order to keep it fresh, and as a consequence her creative process is very different every time. Inspiration can range from modern life to social and scientific developments. She describes her customer as 'curious and headstrong, looking for a quality in design that lies beyond trends'.

www.pelicanavenue.com

1. Printed rain poncho, 'Day-01', S/S 07. 2. 'Ousted' video still, shown as background at Remix Vienna, 2007. 3–4. Printed rain pullovers, S/S 07. 5. Digital-print blouse, Remix Vienna, 2007. 6–7. Knitted jacquard jacket and velvet trousers; hand embroidered t-shirt. 'Ousted', A/W 07. 8. Embroidered and printed family crests, 'Erben', S/S 06. 9. Digital-print jacket and leggings, Remix Vienna, 2007.

4

*Looking for a quality in design
that lies beyond trends*
___**Pelican Avenue**

5

6

7

8

9

1

2

3

'My work is a radical subjective reflection of reality from the corner of an outsider's eye,' explains Bulgarian designer Petar Petrov. Moving to Austria in 1999, Petrov studied under the renowned fashion designer Raf Simons at the University of Applied Arts Vienna.

Petar Petrov___72/100

In 2003 Petrov won the Unit F award for international press, which gave him a press office to promote his brand internationally. Then, as a member of the fashion class at the University of Applied Arts, he was chosen for the Moët & Chandon award for fashion schools at the Swiss fashion event GWAND in Lucerne. Petrov has also worked for Wendy & Jim, where he was responsible for the production and presentation of the Autumn/Winter 00/01 menswear collection.

Petrov presented his first menswear collection, Spring/Summer 03, at Paris Men's Fashion Week. He describes his collections as an extension of himself: 'They come from the selected pieces I make, so every piece is part of the concept and every piece is part of myself somehow.'

Working with self-evident things and traditional elements inspires Petrov. Using his Eastern European roots as reflections in his work, Petrov focuses on experimentation and the development of his work, making sure he is free in his inspirations, influences and intentions. 'My collections have the role to provoke, to raise questions in the audience,' he explains. 'There is no predetermined meaning, but meaning gleaned from the experience of the encounter. The encounter is my interest, not the meaning.'

www.petarpetrov.com

1. White mesh and patent leather jacket with jersey leggings, S/S 08. 2. Black leather gloves, A/W 07. 3. Bleached sweatshirt and mustard jeans with side-zipped grey gussets, S/S 07. 4. Photoshoot, A/W 04. 5. Backstage at the A/W 07 show. 6. Beige jacket and trousers with openwork-detail jumper and dinner shirt, S/S 07. 7. Lycra suit with matching top and shoes, A/W 05. 8. Silver satin bomber and black turtle neck, A/W 06.

'My collections have the role to provoke, to raise questions in the audience'
___**Petar Petrov**

5

6

7

Born in Germany to Russian immigrants, Peter Bertsch studied at the Royal Academy of Fine Arts in Antwerp. After undertaking work placements as a tailor and patternmaker, he showed his graduation collection, 'Bionic', in 2006. The collection was inspired by society's desire to present physical perfection and the trend for optimizing appearance through excessive sport, cosmetics, body transformations and plastic surgery. The collection won the Anne Chapelle Award, the Beck's Fashion Award and the Lancôme Colour Design Award. In 2007 he also won the 1.2.3 Award at the Festival International des Arts de la Mode in Hyères, France.

Peter Bertsch___*73/100*

Describing his design philosophy as the science of beauty, Bertsch says, 'I like to work very scientifically. I can conduct research for ages. I am always interested in the psychology and the background of something. Sometimes you won't see the connection to fashion any more because it is so abstract. But then I start translating it into clothes and you can feel the tension and the story behind it'. Bertsch finds researching a collection to be a very beautiful and intimate experience: 'The moment when you let it out on stage is comparable to a birth, with all the fears and the relief.'

Bertsch enjoys creating sharp contrasts between materials and colour to create tension. He thrives on translating feelings into garments, without interfering with the clothes' function of covering the body. He considers there to be 'new movements in design and new reasons for simply creating. I believe we are at a very good point in time, where something new will happen – not just in fashion but in our society in general.'

Key to Bertsch's work is continuous research and his search to invent new techniques and materials. He believes that during the last twenty years the advances in the textile sector have been rather limited, explaining, 'I have a lot of dreams of qualities you should be able to achieve in a garment'. Bertsch's creative approach to design produces garments that are considered both beautiful and challenging.

1. Quilted patchwork dress and astronaut jacket, 'I Love', A/W 06. 2. PVC mask, collaboration with Elvis Pompillio, 'Bionic'. S/S 07. 3. Dress and astronaut jacket photographed for *Pulp* magazine, A/W 06. 4. PVC and wood shoes, S/S 07. 5. Metallic wrap-dress with PVC details, S/S 07. 6–9. Transparent velvet coat; metallic dress; neoprene suit; orchid jacket with copper-coated leather skirt. 'Bionic', S/S 07.

PETER BERTSCH

4

5

'I have a lot of dreams of qualities you should be able to achieve in a garment'
___**Peter Bertsch**

7

9

1

2

3

Before studying fashion at the Royal Academy of Fine Arts in Antwerp, Belgium, Austrian-born Peter Pilotto worked in London for three years as a window-dresser for Vivienne Westwood. Graduating in 2004, he was hailed as the most promising student in his class. His graduate collection, 'Carried Away by a Moonlight Shadow', was inspired by the clothing and lifestyle of Sinti and Roma gypsies and was recognized by the Flanders Fashion Institute, winning several awards including the Coccodrillo Shoe Award, the Maria Luisa Award and the Unit F Award.

Peter Pilotto____74/100

'I am a very visual thinker and therefore I try to express things in a visual way,' states Pilotto. 'I love to play with atmospheres and meanings but I refuse to explain them. I prefer the viewer to do that.' Pilotto's clothes are described as poetic, energetic, avant-garde and elegant. They are usually extravagantly decorated designs filled with evocative imagery. The garments purposely leave room for many associations and interpretations and allow for the free play of identities. The designer's refusal to explain their context only adds to their magical appeal.

Pilotto's mystically-inspired world of ideas is also apparent in his first video installation, which was exhibited at the Window Gallery of Walter Van Beirendonck, Antwerp, in December 2004 and subsequently at the cultural centre in Andratx in May 2005.

Pilotto describes contemporary fashion as 'chaos' because it is a challenge to be personal and fashionable at the same time. He imagines his customers as 'ageless, elegant, interested, independent, and those that dare to wear'.

For Pilotto, the most enjoyable part of the design process is when elements of different inspirations start to interlink: 'I see things that inspire me and start to imagine them in my translation. I am inspired by Léon Bakst (the Russian painter and Ballets Russes designer and illustrator), clockwork, medieval pageboys, Paul Poiret, science fiction, deserts, the Wiener Werkstätte, phone cables, Ancient Rome and Egypt, time machines, any media, museums, places and friends.'

www.peterpilotto.com

1. Plastic patchwork top with viscose net top and paper earrings, graduate collection 2004. 2–3. Pleated bustier; bustier with pleated tulip skirt, S/S 08. 4. 'Time Machine' artwork, A/W 07. 5–8. Printed silk dress with spiral-cable accessories; printed stockings and top with cable accessories; printed silk top and skirt; printed viscose dress. All S/S 07. 9. Midnight printed silk coat, graduate collection. 10. Printed jacket and tights, S/S 08.

5

'I love to play with atmospheres and meanings but I refuse to explain them'___**Peter Pilotto**

7

8

9

10

1

2

3

German designers Eva Postweiler and Raphael Hauber founded Postweiler Hauber in 2003. Both studied fashion design at HFG Pforzheim in Germany, graduating in 2003, and both had solo exhibitions at the Museum Quarter, Vienna, curated by the Austrian design duo Wendy & Jim.

Postweiler Hauber___*75/100*

In March 2004 *Postweiler Hauber* debuted their first collection, 'Because the Middle is Inside', in Paris. All their collections are created for both men and women but with an emphasis on menswear. Their interest lies in change, as they see fashion as the distillation of new ideas that have not been described before in a product. 'We find inspiration in everyday life,' explains Hauber. 'Weird people with original lifestyles are good for inspiration as well as theoretical and abstract fields. Things that are untreated and authentic or the absurd and artificial, are inspirations that repulse or attract me.' Their aesthetic is clean, sober and contemporary.

The glam rock and nightlife of the 1970s informed their Spring/Summer 06 collection, 'The Night in Your Mind'. Using materials such as silk Lurex, Lycra and a glossy cotton mélange of metallic gold and turquoise, the pair created a collection with an inherently modern aesthetic. The team enjoy researching the beginning of a collection, but the high point is realizing the finished garment. Hauber explains, 'It is interesting to see the subtle unconscious changes for the better that have occurred between the original idea and the completed garment.'

Postweiler Hauber focuses on youth and the clothes appeal to individuals with spirit, 'People with similar feelings for the environment, who understand the spirit of the collection. Mostly they are young or young at heart, open-minded with a big interest in fashion, art and music.' Retaining an intuitive feeling for what is really modern is essential to the concept, and Hauber believes that 'something is only modern when other people also have a similarly true feeling about its modernity'.

www.postweilerhauber.com

1. Folded white t-shirt from 'I love my t' show invitation, S/S 07. 2. Cover for A/W 04 Lookbook, 'Because the Middle is Inside'. 3. Black and white cycling shorts with mesh inserts, 'Copyshop', S/S 08. 4. Lacquered jogging bottoms, S/S 08. 5–12. Lookbook cover showing garments from 'der Blaue Reiter', A/W 06. 13. Grey and black denim shirt and jeans with metallic pendant necklace, 'Completed', A/W 07. 14. Oversized 'Tandem' sweater, S/S 08.

4

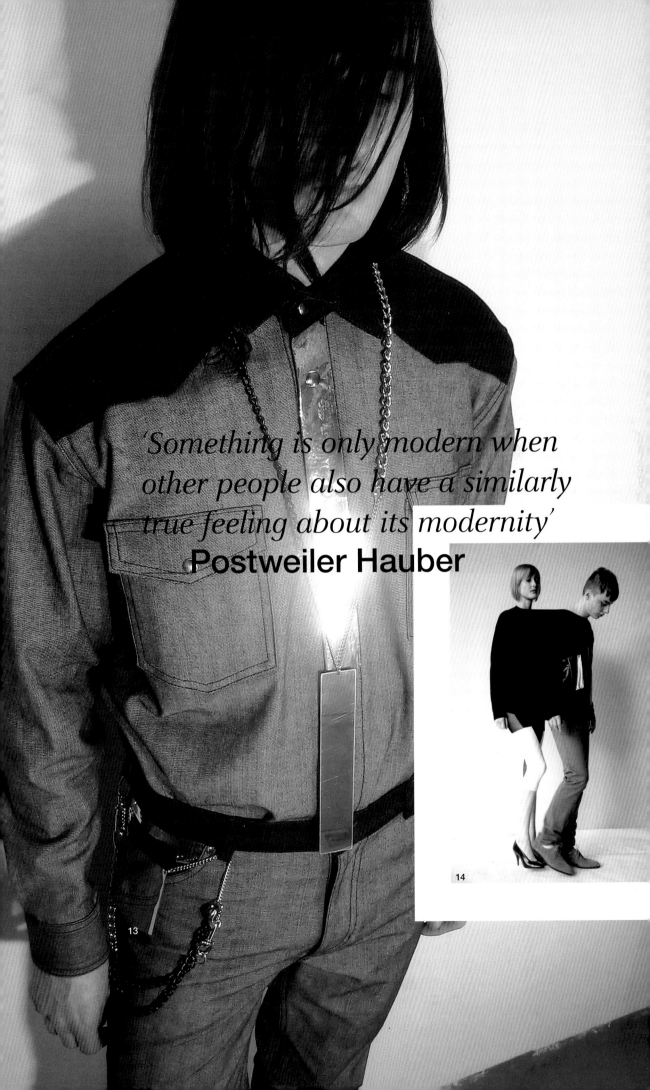

'Something is only modern when other people also have a similarly true feeling about its modernity'
Postweiler Hauber

13

14

1

3

4

PPQ started life as a fashion, music and arts collective involved in numerous projects including London club nights, collaborations with Sam Taylor-Wood and Gary Hume, a recording studio and a record label (1234 Records). Amy Molyneaux and Percy Parker launched PPQ clothing in Spring/Summer 2000. In 2006 the designers opened a flagship store in London, and its modish interior exemplified PPQ's luxurious but irreverent design aesthetic.

PPQ___76/100

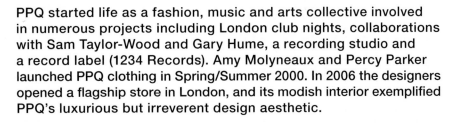

Originally accredited with influencing the drainpipe revolution, *PPQ* is also known for its signature smock-shaped and jewel-coloured cocktail dresses. Being both aesthetically and commercially astute, *PPQ* sell their range in boutiques across Europe and in Japan. With an investment from Icelandic retail giants Baugur, the label is admired within the British Fashion Industry for successfully combining commercialism with creativity.

Describe your design philosophy. *PPQ is a lifestyle; the colours and shapes we create come from and inspire the way we live, and the music we make is another dimension of this.*

How would you define your aesthetic? *We impose no boundaries on where we go with our ideas.*

What is the most enjoyable part of design? *Having the ideas and knowing you can't control when they come.*

How would you describe your customer? *PPQ customers are both new- and old-guard rock and roll.*

How would you describe your creative process? *Our creative process is never-ending and always evolving. Design is our life, not a job.*

How would you define contemporary fashion? *Contemporary fashion is a moment in your mind where you feel in tune with the mood a garment evokes; this could be vintage or new – it's an attitude.*

Who or what informs your work? *Our lives inspire us, the people we meet and the places we go.*

What is the most challenging aspect of design? *Having enough time to do all the things we want to do.*

How are you personally innovative in fashion design? *We design with good times in mind, so our shapes and colours always have a futuristic yet culturally relevant feeling to them. It makes our customers feel like they are in a groove and connect with PPQ.*

www.ppqclothing.com

1. Printed 'Michel' mini-dress with flared sleeves, A/W 04. **2.** 'Estella' ruffle-detail dress, S/S 07. **3.** Gold taffeta 'Fuzzious' dress with sculpted sleeves, A/W 07. **4.** Vibrant silk-satin 'Opal' short suit with sash, A/W 06. **4.** Design sketches, S/S 08.

1

2

Founded by Elisabeth Schotte, Franziska Schreiber, Therese Pfeil and Franziska Piefke in 2003, PULVER is a creative collective that aims to express the founders' shared vision of womenswear. The collective's concept unites the designers' diverse influences to create a collection that is complex but balanced.

PULVER___*77/100*

How would you define your aesthetic? *PULVER unites an effortlessly elegant style with an elaborate cut and detail. A collection that easily becomes one's own favourite pieces.*

What is the most enjoyable part of design? *When the first samples arrive and you get an idea of what the collection is going to be like. Everything falls into place and decisions can be made.*

How would you describe your customer? *Elegant and tough, women who love to combine and play with designs.*

How would you describe your creative process? *The design process is accompanied by research and debate of a concept often inspired by a fictional or real person. The main objective is always to make women feel and look good and confident in each piece. We strive to make contact with creative people from all disciplines for the development of our collections and presentations.*

How would you define contemporary fashion? *Fashion that makes you feel good in the moment that it is worn.*

Who or what informs your work? *The design team is inspired by diverse sources, including people in the street, magazines, books, fabrics, old costumes and even menswear design.*

What is the most challenging aspect of design? *To create a whole world with each collection – from the pieces in the collection to the look book, the show and everything.*

www.pulver-studio.de

1. Cabled coat, 'Margarite and the Master', A/W 07. 2. Dress, 'Scarlett', A/W 05. 3. Shot from 'To the Stars' campaign, S/S 05. 4–8. Clean, classic separates utilize a monochrome palette, 'Utopia', S/S 08.

3

4

'The main objective is always to make women feel and look good and confident in each piece'

___**PULVER**

6

1   2

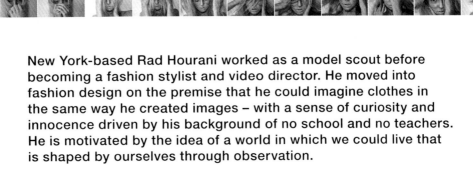

New York-based Rad Hourani worked as a model scout before becoming a fashion stylist and video director. He moved into fashion design on the premise that he could imagine clothes in the same way he created images – with a sense of curiosity and innocence driven by his background of no school and no teachers. He is motivated by the idea of a world in which we could live that is shaped by ourselves through observation.

Rad Hourani____*78/100*

Hourani describes his clothes as 'asexual, "aseasonal", coming from no place, no time and no tradition'. Drawing on a monochromatic and graphic canvas with a palette of blacks and touches of pure whites and intense reds, the collections present sophisticated modern classics for anti-conformist individuals.

Describe your design philosophy. *I design from a very virgin point of view, trying to elude classical ready-to-wear rules that make us believe that women and men deserve different approaches.*

How would you define your aesthetic? *Straight. Sharp. Slick.*

How would you describe your creative process? *There is no specific process. I just carry a mental notebook in which I make notes at any time of the day. I can be inspired by someone on the street, by a book or by a discussion. Then I put it into a few straight lines.*

How would you define contemporary fashion? *Like contemporary times: dark and serious with a dash of flamboyance and self-indulgence.*

Who or what informs your work? *Anything from how my lunch looks on my plate to a piece of electro rock music.*

What is the most challenging aspect of design? *The same challenge as any language: to be understood and to make people react to what you say, whatever that reaction might be. There's nothing scarier than making fashion – or anything else, for that matter – that everybody agrees on.*

How are you personally innovative in fashion design? *To be innovative for the sake of innovation is not my cup of tea. I hope I'll be able to design from a free angle at all times. But that story is still unwritten, I guess...*

www.radhourani.com

1–2. Silk dress, silver necklace and stretch cotton-silk pants; leather vest with silk top and stretch jeans. S/S 08. **3.** Model shots for MODE 20 Expo for Rad Hourani, S/S 08 collection.

3

1

2

'Layered, feminine and functional clothes' are at the heart of Raeburn Design, a partnership between brothers Christopher and Graeme Raeburn. Both studied at Middlesex University and then at the Royal College of Art, with Graeme graduating in 2003 and Christopher in 2006.

Raeburn Design___*79/100*

Focusing on functional beauty in a twenty-first-century cityscape, the designers produce collections inspired by modern, nomadic lifestyles, clothing for extreme weathers and the functionality of military clothing. 'Everything has a reason' is a key motto at *Raeburn Design*. 'Clothing is the initial point of judgment and contact for most people; we like to explore this twilight zone, often building layers and depth into an outfit or garment to be used at will by the wearer. A game of hide-and-seek, of sexuality, strength, imagination and intelligence that allows the wearer's physical representation to be at one with their state of mind.'

The design team takes inspiration from silhouettes and details borne out of extreme environments or function-specific clothing. The garments often rejuvenate surplus materials and in so doing reinterpret existing seams and features, creating a piece with a history beyond its own. 'We love to integrate "passive features", such as specific-use hidden pockets or a degree of adjustability, to enable the user to effortlessly adapt and interact with different environments and situations.'

For the brothers, the most enjoyable part of design is seeing someone wearing their clothes in the street. They also appreciate that the design journey can be very powerful – having the skills to take a design from an embryonic sketch through to a finished garment is incredibly satisfying. They describe their creative process as 'always fun, slightly reckless, often misdirected, optimistic, a constant fight for time, sometimes like a slow-motion punch-up in an army jumble sale, full-throttle, thoughtful and considered although often instinctive. Tiring, exhilarating, conclusive and yet desperate for more.'

www.raeburndesign.co.uk

1–3. Digital-print pleated skirt with leather accessory bag; silk-chiffon layered coat with digital-print pleated skirt; oversized parka. All 'Godspeed', A/W 07. **4–5.** Silk-devoré bias-cut dress with silk-jersey underdress and cylinder handbag; design sketches of the outfit. 'Where Nighthawks Fly', S/S 06. **6.** Cropped jacket and high-waisted shorts with accessories by Raeburn Design, 'Schneertarn', S/S 08. **7.** Silk-chiffon backless jacket with jersey digital-print dress, A/W 07.

3

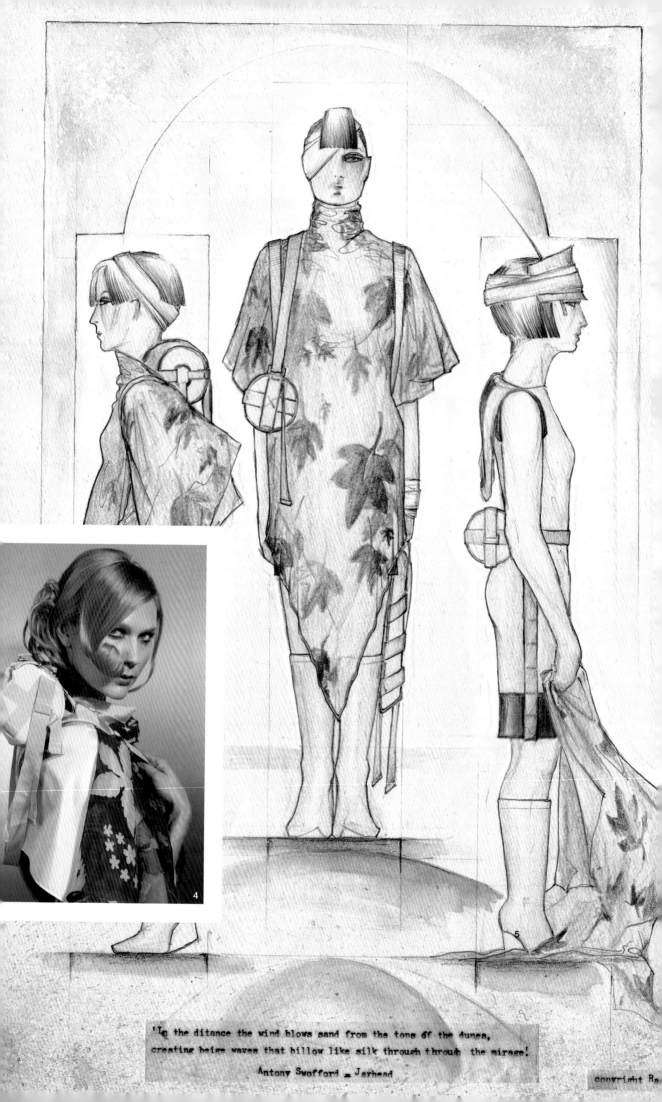

'In the ditance the wind blows sand from the tops of the dunes,
creating beige waves that billow like silk through through the mirage!

Antony Swofford - Jarhead

'Everything has a reason'
___Raeburn Design

1

2

In 2002 Richard Nicoll graduated with an MA from Central Saint Martins. His final year collection was bought by Dolce & Gabbana, and since then the British-born, Australian-raised designer has worked for Louis Vuitton as well as presenting his own collections at London Fashion Week.

Richard Nicoll___*80/100*

Nicoll's signature style combines menswear fabrics with corsetry and couture detailing to create strong, sculpted garments. His collections celebrate idiosyncratic personal style over status and overt sexuality.

Describe your design philosophy. *I'm interested in people as unique characters rather than as physical commodities. I make a lot of separates rather than dresses because my favourite thing is to see people who wear my clothes by mixing them with their own style. I'm just really inspired by individuals and not so much homogenized style.*

What is the most enjoyable part of design? *The research: establishing the mood and look of the collection and then seeing it come to life at the show. I love seeing this army of characters that I've created lining up backstage. I guess it's a small bit of momentary Utopia.*

How would you describe your creative process? *It is pretty painful and manic. I have moments of pure excitement and then periods of sheer panic. I normally go through designing about three or four collections before I get to one that I'm happy with. When I hear the soundtrack that feels right for the show is when I really define the collection and get excited.*

Who or what informs your work? *I'm inspired and informed by music, smart friends, certain moods and fleeting emotions, cute and unusual personalities, art and dance.*

How are you personally innovative in fashion design? *By following my instinct and by being myself. It's easy to compromise your true style according to what you know people want to see. Fashion is like a dialect – once you understand how it works, it's easy to take a shortcut to success because you know what is coming next. But I think it's important to take the long road and to create your own aesthetic, not to follow the crowd.*

www.richardnicoll.com

1. Ruffle blouse and cargo shorts, S/S 06. 2. Draped silk twill dress, S/S 06. 3. Inspirations collage. 4. Portrait of Ossie Clark by Richard Nicholl. 5–8. Spot linen jacket with silk blouse and printed leather bloomers; cotton playsuit with silk scarf attached; silk oyster trousers; draped spot-print silk dress with orange underskirt. S/S 07. 9. Striped gabardine bra with cotton chino paperbag trousers, S/S 06. 10. Draped baby-cord dress with wooden bead, A/W 05.

3

'I'm interested in people as unique characters rather than as physical commodities' ___**Richard Nicoll**

5

4

7

8

9

10

At the age of 20, Robert Normand graduated from Studio Berçot in Paris. He specialized in knitwear design, collaborating with Christophe Lemaire, Hervé Léger and Ocimar Versolato, and later working for Lanvin, Lacoste and Emilio Pucci. With these collaborations, his reputation for excellence was firmly established, and in 2000 he launched his own ready-to-wear collection.

Robert Normand___*81/100*

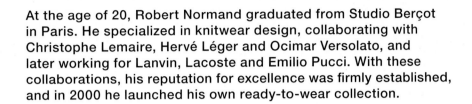

Contemporary lightweight knits, delicate prints and soft blouson shapes are trademarks of Normand's collections. His own family origins are culturally diverse, and influences from France, Germany, North Africa, Brazil and Japan inform his work. His style is a mix of traditional craftsmanship and contemporary attitude and Normand regularly works with artists, illustrators and graphic artists to give his collection new perspectives.

Describe your design philosophy. *A casual preciousness – like a t-shirt dress from the nineteenth century.*

How would you define your aesthetic? *I try to gather together my contradictions: romantic/tough, cheesy/intellectual, draped/tailored.*

What is the most enjoyable part of design? *Meeting people and sharing ideas.*

How would you describe your customer? *I don't think about age. I would like to dress women who are fond of culture and art. Women with strong characters who go for something different, eccentric yet intelligent.*

How would you describe your creative process? *I devour lots of images, digest them slowly and make a colourful collage.*

How would you define contemporary fashion? *It's too broad to be defined. Everyone has the potential to express themselves through clothing, whatever their budget or physique, but it is difficult for most people to find themselves when faced with such a huge choice.*

Who or what informs your work? *Art, interior design, vintage fashion and music videos: the usual things, but seen through my lens.*

What is the most challenging aspect of design? *Reaching the right girl on the right spot at the right moment, and, if possible, with the right music in the air.*

How are you personally innovative in fashion design? *Every human being has a special story. Starting with a general view of my past, I hope to be able to define something personal and therefore different and perhaps interesting.*

www.robertnormand.com

1. Artwork by Emmanuelle Mafille, A/W 01. **2–3.** Sleeveless dress; top with 'Mechanic' print by Ludivine Billaud. All A/W 06. **4.** Pic-nic print by Amélie Charroin, invitation for S/S 07 show. **5.** Jacket and skirt featuring 'COQ' print by Anamorphée, A/W 05. **6.** Sleeveless top with gathered bottom, S/S 07. **7.** Striped top, A/W 06.

5

6

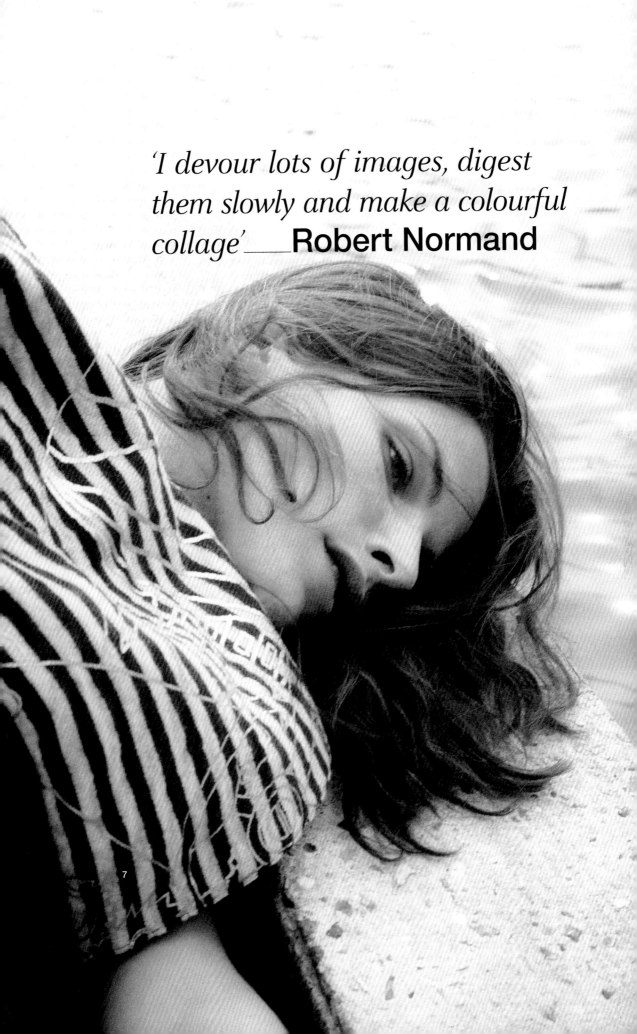

*'I devour lots of images, digest them slowly and make a colourful collage'*___**Robert Normand**

7

1

2

Athens-born Romina Karamanea moved to the UK in 1995 where she studied fashion design and product development at Nottingham Trent University. She went on to Central Saint Martins in London to take a postgraduate diploma in innovative pattern-cutting. After graduating, Karamanea worked for Clements Ribeiro, Robert Cary-Williams, Marcus Lupfer and Preen before launching her own label in 2005. Described by the fashion press as the 'goddess of intellectual clothing', Karamanea uses cut and proportion so that every drape, silhouette and stitch has a purpose and a place.

Romina Karamanea___*82/100*

Describe your design philosophy. *Technical discipline combined with creative freedom, gained by studying in-depth history and by being true to the classical design process.*

How would you define your aesthetic? *An appreciation of balanced proportions, shade and shape. I would describe it as an internal battle of all the things that move me and things that I hate, so my aesthetic is more about cause and effect rather than comfortable definitions of what is beautiful.*

What is the most enjoyable part of design? *I would definitely say that special moment where suddenly all the chaos and infinite choices that wouldn't let me sleep for days come together effortlessly.*

How would you describe your customer? *A person who possesses power and elegance with a hidden sensual side.*

How would you describe your creative process? *Design is evident everywhere I look. The creative process is in living my everyday routine and observing even the most unspectacular things that I come across.*

What is the most challenging aspect of design? *Decision-making. When you have to realize and understand that every choice you make, from the most insignificant to the most important, will follow you through every step of the process. Also, taking for granted that mistakes will happen and approaching them as learning opportunities.*

www.rominakaramanea.com

1. Black wool skirt, A/W 07. 2. Silk tasar dress, S/S 07. 3. Dress in toile development stage, S/S 09. 4. Silk tie-die dress with Swarovski crystals, S/S 06. 5. Cashmere jacket with lace shorts, A/W 06. 6. Wool coat, A/W 07. 7. Cotton and silk-chiffon dress, S/S 08.

3

4

5

'The creative process is in living my everyday routine and observing even the most unspectacular things that I come across'
___**Romina Karamanea**

7

6

1

2

Born in The Netherlands, Romy Smits has lived most of her life in Belgium. Despite having never formally studied fashion design she worked as a consultant for Dries Van Noten between 1999 and 2001. She created her first couture concept after being inspired by the shimmering threads in Moroccan souks, and in 2002 presented her first design in knitted viscose, which was purchased by Barneys in New York.

Romy Smits___*83/100*

Since 2002 Smits has worked as an independent designer, and her company, *Kantakari Bvba*, has become a contemporary design studio for concepts in fashion, interior design, textiles and art. Her work is defined by innovative concepts, symbolic images and personal styling, and she combines modernism with authenticity. Smits sees her artistic inspiration and creativity as being in harmony with the natural universe, explaining, 'I aim to depict the very fine line between intuition and shape, which connects emotions and objects.'

For Smits, the creative process begins with draping fabrics to see immediately whether or not she likes a certain direction. The freedom to play without knowing the outcome is very important, and her inspiration comes from her 'inner self, the cosmos and the spiritual'. Smits sees her biggest challenge as being 'to rediscover myself every time I create something and to find out what else I can do without limiting myself'. With this in mind, she creates subtle modern shapes informed by emotions and life experience.

Shunning the six-month cycles of the fashion calendar, Smits aims to create clothes that are timeless and enduring, and her handpainted textiles and carefully crafted garments betray her interest in artisan traditions.

www.romysmits.com

1. Handpainted coat, 'White Heat', S/S 06. 2. Knitted viscose dress, 'Radiance', S/S 04. 3. Detail from knitted viscose dress, 'Magic Colours', S/S 03. 4–5. Screen print on cotton; screen print on viscose lycra. 'Soul of Africa', S/S 05. 6. Digital prints on textiles and PVC, 'Citrien', S/S 07.

3

4

5

'I aim to depict the very fine line between intuition and shape, which connects emotions and objects' __Romy Smits

1

2

Norwegian womenswear designer Hilde Rubecksen and Japanese knitwear designer Tomoko Yamanaka established Rubecksen Yamanaka in 2002. The team met at the Royal College of Art in London and have worked together ever since. In 2003 Rubecksen Yamanaka won the British Craft Council's business development award, and in 2004 they were one of four finalists in Fashion Fringe, the UK fashion design competition. The fusion of their different cultures has produced a distinctive look that is entirely their own.

Rubecksen Yamanaka
___84/100

Describe your design philosophy. *Timeless, ageless and simple.*

How would you define your aesthetic? *Beautifully peculiar.*

What is the most enjoyable part of design? *Selecting yarns and fabrics and the feeling you get when you create something that is just right.*

How would you describe your customer? *Someone who appreciates quality and classical but quirky design.*

How would you describe your creative process? *We take a detail or object out of its usual context and place it somewhere else. In many ways it is also like cooking a nice meal.*

How would you define contemporary fashion? *For us, contemporary fashion embraces elements from the past and uses materials that have integrity and worth.*

Who or what informs your work? *Everyday objects and events, vintage clothing and Victorian photography inspire us, and artists like Louise Bourgeois and Hans Bellmer. Inspiration is quite mixed but the aesthetic is always of a similar kind whether it is historic or current.*

What is the most challenging aspect of design? *To be cost-efficient.*

How are you personally innovative in fashion design? *We don't aim to be innovative and modern. We just are who we are and aim to design what we want to wear.*

www.rubecksenyamanaka.com

1–2. Linen jacket and sailor shorts; twinset and shoelace-linen skirt. S/S 07. **3.** Handknit muff jumper, A/W 07. **4–7.** Cotton pleat dress; glove scarf; six-finger gloves; camel long johns. A/W 05. **8.** Sheer cotton dress with ruched sleeve detail. **9.** Cashmere mitten scarf, A/W 07.

3

4

'We take a detail or object out of its usual context and place it somewhere else'
___Rubecksen Yamanaka

6

8

9

1

2

Graduating from ESMOD in Tokyo in 2001, Seïko Taki went on to study for a diploma in cutting at the Academie Internationale de Coupe in Paris. She then studied dress design, also in Paris. From 2003 until 2006 Taki was fashion stylist to Anne Valérie Hash before presenting her first collection and launching the Seïko Taki brand in 2007. The label's aesthetic is based on the designer's female ideal: a woman who is both youthful and childish.

Seïko Taki___*85/100*

Describe your design philosophy. *Natural rock.*

How would you define your aesthetic? *The ultimate beauty would be a naked human being.*

What is the most enjoyable part of design? *When I create something new and original.*

How would you describe your customer? *A person who has a unique personality.*

How would you describe your creative process? *I do not have a process. I do everything at the same time. I want to create clothes that are as simple as possible, as strong as possible, as efficient as possible, in a short time.*

How would you define contemporary fashion? *I am very sad because there is too much emphasis on business.*

Who or what informs your work? *Nature. In addition, all the friends who support me – their energy and their love become my flesh and blood, which gives me power.*

What is the most challenging aspect of design? *To concentrate on the ultimate line. Not to make any compromises and to face myself. To respect the balance with business. I do not think design is about doing as one pleases. Good design lives forever: it outstrips time.*

How are you personally innovative in fashion design? *By facing nature.*

www.seiko-taki-paris.com

1. Shortsleeve drawstring bolero blouse and brown shirt with frilled collar, slim trousers and felt hat, A/W 07. 2. Leather biker jacket and tulle negligee with ruffled trousers and knitted hat, S/S 08. 3. Silk blouse with frilled collar and polyester tank top, A/W 07. 4–7. Ruffled silk evening gown and white linen slip dress; white drawstring dress with wrap-around skirt worn as dress and felt hat; mohair scarf and cardigan with shiny drawstring-bottom trousers; jacket with lace detail, organza shirt, ruffled-hem skirt and felt hat. All A/W 07. 8. Sleeveless leather biker jacket with cream shirt and black trousers, S/S 08. 9. Black mohair muffler and polyester tank top, A/W 07.

3

'The ultimate beauty would be a naked human being'
Seïko Taki

9

8

2

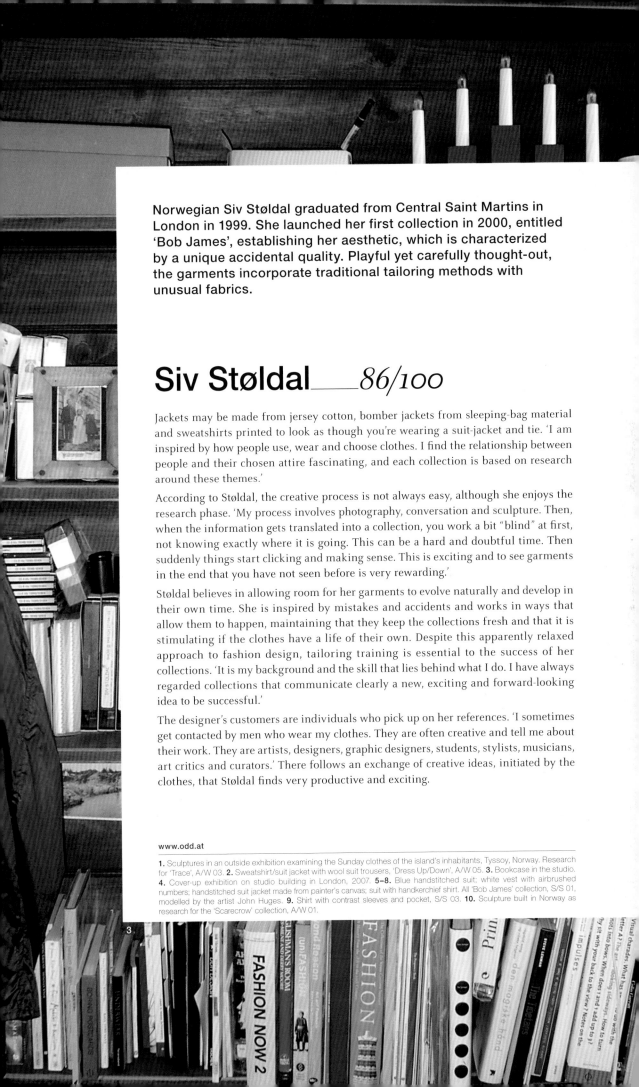

Norwegian Siv Støldal graduated from Central Saint Martins in London in 1999. She launched her first collection in 2000, entitled 'Bob James', establishing her aesthetic, which is characterized by a unique accidental quality. Playful yet carefully thought-out, the garments incorporate traditional tailoring methods with unusual fabrics.

Siv Støldal___*86/100*

Jackets may be made from jersey cotton, bomber jackets from sleeping-bag material and sweatshirts printed to look as though you're wearing a suit-jacket and tie. 'I am inspired by how people use, wear and choose clothes. I find the relationship between people and their chosen attire fascinating, and each collection is based on research around these themes.'

According to Støldal, the creative process is not always easy, although she enjoys the research phase. 'My process involves photography, conversation and sculpture. Then, when the information gets translated into a collection, you work a bit "blind" at first, not knowing exactly where it is going. This can be a hard and doubtful time. Then suddenly things start clicking and making sense. This is exciting and to see garments in the end that you have not seen before is very rewarding.'

Støldal believes in allowing room for her garments to evolve naturally and develop in their own time. She is inspired by mistakes and accidents and works in ways that allow them to happen, maintaining that they keep the collections fresh and that it is stimulating if the clothes have a life of their own. Despite this apparently relaxed approach to fashion design, tailoring training is essential to the success of her collections. 'It is my background and the skill that lies behind what I do. I have always regarded collections that communicate clearly a new, exciting and forward-looking idea to be successful.'

The designer's customers are individuals who pick up on her references. 'I sometimes get contacted by men who wear my clothes. They are often creative and tell me about their work. They are artists, designers, graphic designers, students, stylists, musicians, art critics and curators.' There follows an exchange of creative ideas, initiated by the clothes, that Støldal finds very productive and exciting.

www.odd.at

1. Sculptures in an outside exhibition examining the Sunday clothes of the island's inhabitants, Tyssoy, Norway. Research for 'Trace', A/W 03. 2. Sweatshirt/suit jacket with wool suit trousers, 'Dress Up/Down', A/W 05. 3. Bookcase in the studio. 4. Cover-up exhibition on studio building in London, 2007. 5–8. Blue handstitched suit; white vest with airbrushed numbers; handstitched suit jacket made from painter's canvas; suit with handkerchief shirt. All 'Bob James' collection, S/S 01, modelled by the artist John Huges. 9. Shirt with contrast sleeves and pocket, S/S 03. 10. Sculpture built in Norway as research for the 'Scarecrow' collection, A/W 01.

5

4

7

8

'*My process involves photography,*
conversation and sculpture'
___Siv Støldal

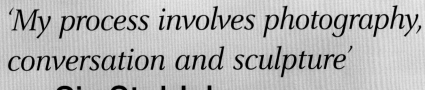

9

10

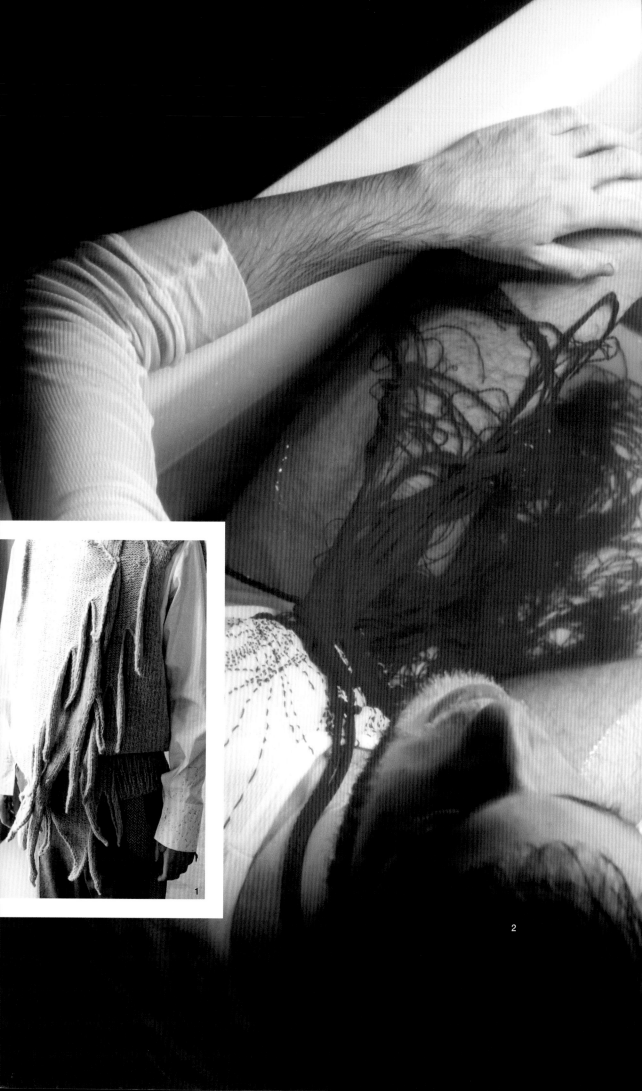

1

2

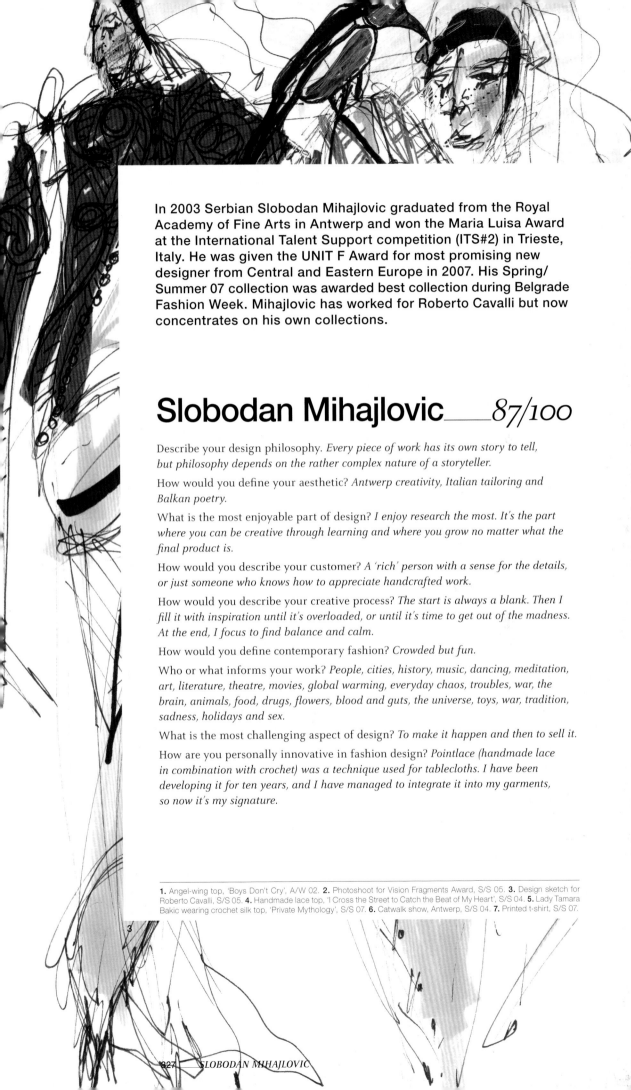

In 2003 Serbian Slobodan Mihajlovic graduated from the Royal Academy of Fine Arts in Antwerp and won the Maria Luisa Award at the International Talent Support competition (ITS#2) in Trieste, Italy. He was given the UNIT F Award for most promising new designer from Central and Eastern Europe in 2007. His Spring/Summer 07 collection was awarded best collection during Belgrade Fashion Week. Mihajlovic has worked for Roberto Cavalli but now concentrates on his own collections.

Slobodan Mihajlovic___*87/100*

Describe your design philosophy. *Every piece of work has its own story to tell, but philosophy depends on the rather complex nature of a storyteller.*

How would you define your aesthetic? *Antwerp creativity, Italian tailoring and Balkan poetry.*

What is the most enjoyable part of design? *I enjoy research the most. It's the part where you can be creative through learning and where you grow no matter what the final product is.*

How would you describe your customer? *A 'rich' person with a sense for the details, or just someone who knows how to appreciate handcrafted work.*

How would you describe your creative process? *The start is always a blank. Then I fill it with inspiration until it's overloaded, or until it's time to get out of the madness. At the end, I focus to find balance and calm.*

How would you define contemporary fashion? *Crowded but fun.*

Who or what informs your work? *People, cities, history, music, dancing, meditation, art, literature, theatre, movies, global warming, everyday chaos, troubles, war, the brain, animals, food, drugs, flowers, blood and guts, the universe, toys, war, tradition, sadness, holidays and sex.*

What is the most challenging aspect of design? *To make it happen and then to sell it.*

How are you personally innovative in fashion design? *Pointlace (handmade lace in combination with crochet) was a technique used for tablecloths. I have been developing it for ten years, and I have managed to integrate it into my garments, so now it's my signature.*

1. Angel-wing top, 'Boys Don't Cry', A/W 02. **2.** Photoshoot for Vision Fragments Award, S/S 05. **3.** Design sketch for Roberto Cavalli, S/S 05. **4.** Handmade lace top, 'I Cross the Street to Catch the Beat of My Heart', S/S 04. **5.** Lady Tamara Bakic wearing crochet silk top, 'Private Mythology', S/S 07. **6.** Catwalk show, Antwerp, S/S 04. **7.** Printed t-shirt, S/S 07.

4

5

'Antwerp creativity, Italian tailoring and Balkan poetry'
___Slobodan Mihajlovic

6

7

1

2

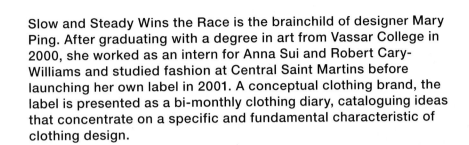

Slow and Steady Wins the Race is the brainchild of designer Mary Ping. After graduating with a degree in art from Vassar College in 2000, she worked as an intern for Anna Sui and Robert Cary-Williams and studied fashion at Central Saint Martins before launching her own label in 2001. A conceptual clothing brand, the label is presented as a bi-monthly clothing diary, cataloguing ideas that concentrate on a specific and fundamental characteristic of clothing design.

Slow and Steady Wins the Race___*88/100*

The concept behind *Slow and Steady Wins the Race* is to produce new designs at a regulated pace throughout the calendar year. This accelerated pace is a commentary on modern fashion's sequential nature. Production costs and quantity are purposefully kept low to help promote the idea of a democratic and grass-roots distribution. The ultimate aim is for ideas and products to reach a wide audience and foster the appreciation and creative progression of clothing design.

With each 'issue' of the clothing diary, Ping intends for the label to 'open up a more democratic dissemination, promotion and appreciation of clothing'. The first issue focused on seams and consisted of six pieces – including a jacket, a tank top and a bag – in 100% cotton that all had design attributes within their seams. Subsequent issues have dealt with print, bags, pockets and underwear. The label's mission is to push and produce interesting and significant pieces from the simplest and most inexpensive fabrics and materials, and the clothes are focused on classic tailoring and intelligent design. Only 100 copies of each issue are produced and only 100 pieces of each style are made.

www.slowandsteadywinstherace.com

1. Cotton-canvas iconic bag, Nº1 'Seams'. **2.** Oxford zip shirt, Nº8 'Shirt'. **3.** Tower design print, Nº2 'Prints'. **4–7.** Sweatshirt with detached sleeves; fleece blazer; funnel-shoulder sweatshirt; poncho with hood. Nº4 'Sweats'. **8.** Hooded sweatshirt blazer, Nº9 'Men'. **9.** Cotton-canvas blazer with exposed seams, Nº1 'Seams'.

3

4

6

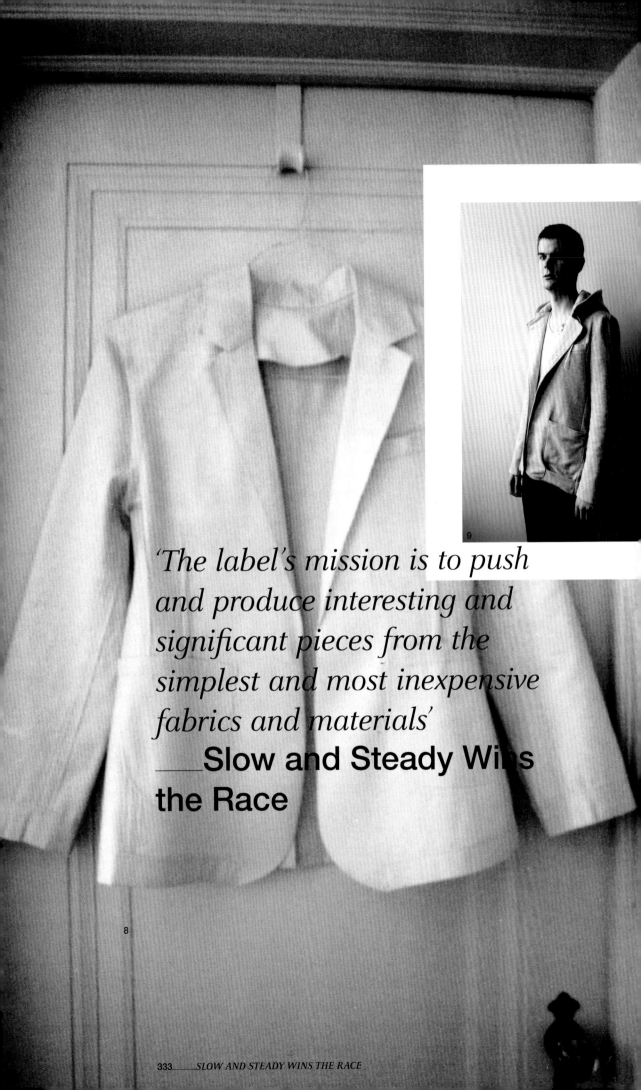

'The label's mission is to push and produce interesting and significant pieces from the simplest and most inexpensive fabrics and materials'

____Slow and Steady Wins the Race

Twin sisters Truus and Riet Spijkers established Spijkers en Spijkers in 2000. After graduating from Arnhem Academy of Art and completing an MA at the Fashion Institute Arnhem, the sisters wanted to build an instantly recognizable and desirable signature style that was sharp, bold and functional.

Spijkers en Spijkers___*89/100*

'Our design philosophy is form follows function. It is partial to the Art Deco and Modern influences of the early 1920s. Decoration should play a functional element or definition in the overall shape of the garment. At the same time functional aspects of the garment are used decoratively. Designs should always be simultaneously avant-garde and wearable.'

While rebelling against stereotypical ideas of femininity, *Spijkers en Spijkers* appeals to modern women. 'We believe our designs speak to confident and active women who rewrite the rules about their sex and sex appeal. The girls we know that wear *Spijkers en Spijkers* are self-conscious and independent thinkers and have their own individual style.'

The twins complement each other's talents. Truus is the painter and thinks in style and colours, while Riet the sculptor turns their ideas into three-dimensional concepts. Citing Elsa Schiaparelli and Madeleine Vionnet as their respective heroines, the pair use their individuality to create their common vision.

Their mix of soft materials with hard lines comes from an ongoing historical fascination with the 1920s, a time they love for its great renewal in the arts, design and attitude. Gathering ideas and being overwhelmed by these ideas is very exciting for the designers. Past collections have been based on detailed explorations of specific historic figures, such as Paul Gauguin's Tahitian mistress Tehura and Picasso's muse Dora Maar.

'We hope our designs reflect our ideas about form, time and emotion and are therefore recognizable as being ours. We want our designs to be innovative but at the same time to have a degree of timelessness.'

www.spijkersenspijkers.com

1. Silk-satin 'Lucy' dress, S/S 05. 2. Patch dress, A/W 07. 3. Shoot for A/W 04 collection. 4. Silk-satin 'Roman' dress, A/W 04. 5–6. Silk-organza butterfly top; silk honan, top and bloomer. S/S 01. 7. Silk-satin 'Eileen' dress, A/W 07.

3

'Designs should always be simultaneously avant-garde and wearable'
___Spijkers en Spijkers

4

5

6

7

Designers Steve Jung and Yoni Pai are graduates of Central Saint Martins and London College of Fashion respectively, and launched their label in 2006. They presented their first collection during London Fashion Week in 2007 and create a contemporary range of both menswear and womenswear. Their debut show drew an impressive audience of national and international buyers and press, and they went on to collaborate with UK fashion chain Topshop to create a diffusion range that was launched in 2007.

Steve J & Yoni P___*90/100*

Their design aesthetic mixes original hand-printed fabrics – graphics on traditional garments – with extreme and sometimes improbable layering. 'Our philosophy is to have the freedom of creation guiding our thoughts and moulding them into the garment that is in our mind,' they explain. 'The most important thing is to keep things in mind and know when it is time to release them. The aim is to find a theme and turn our ideas into a story surrounding it.'

The collections include accessories as well as dresses, suits, knitwear and evening pieces. The designers aim to achieve a blend of coloured and patterned fabrics and to create a balance between extreme couture and ready-to-wear, heritage chic and modern art, juxtaposing traditional tailoring with fantastical inspirations.

For each collection, Jung and Pai decide on a country, culture or theme from which to take ideas and then spend time conducting research, forming visual concepts and sketching their thoughts. They explain how the creation grows through all steps of the design process: 'Your ideas transform into something more of an illusion than you imagined as you discover new colour compositions and, when draping fabric, you find new and unusual folds and beautiful twists.'

Maintaining that they do not have a specific customer in mind, the designers claim 'We design for everyone who wants to express themselves through fashion.' Contemporary fashion, according to Steve Jung and Yoni Pai, is about individuals showing who they are through undefined fashion trends. Being forward-thinking is key to their philosophy, and they want to create trends rather than follow them.

www.stevejandyonip.com

1. Polo-neck knit and fur hat, A/W 07. 2. Tailored linen jacket, white shorts and braided-neckline top, S/S 08. 3. Fabric map, A/W 07. 4. Sheer cotton-jersey top with braided detail, S/S 08. 5. Double-organza off-the-shoulder draped dress, S/S 08. 6. Printed heavy-cotton oversized coat with sheepskin collar, chiffon layered dress and wood hat, A/W 07. 7. Flower decorated chiffon dress, A/W 07. 8. Design sketch by Yoni Pai, A/W 07.

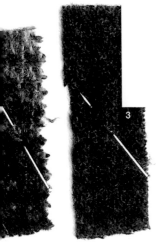
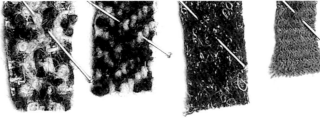

8

'The aim is to find a theme and turn our ideas into a story surrounding it'
___Steve J & Yoni P

7

1

2

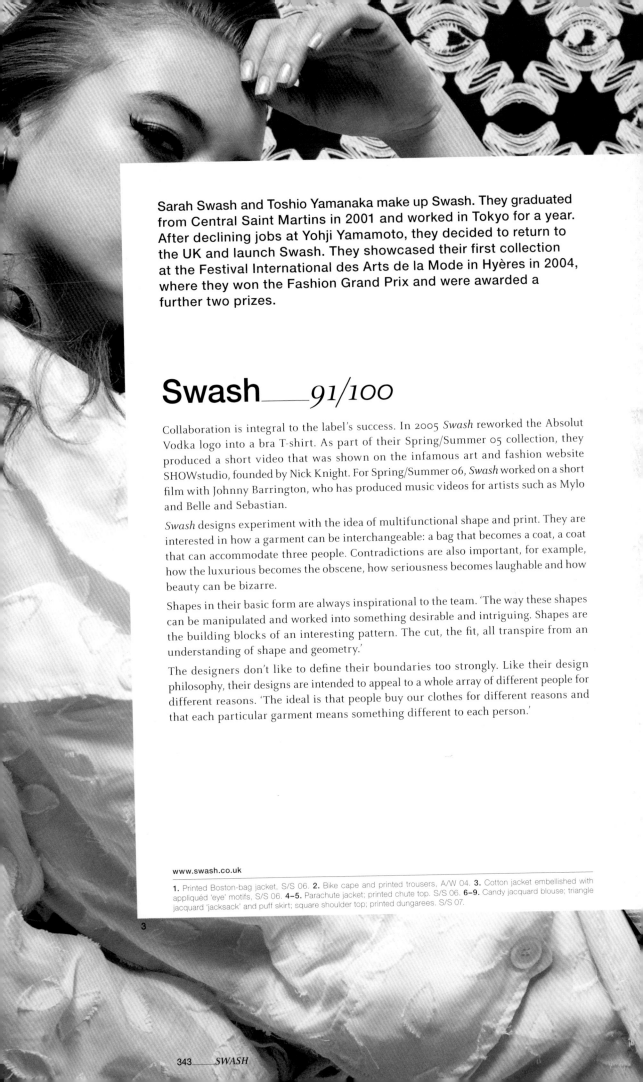

Sarah Swash and Toshio Yamanaka make up Swash. They graduated from Central Saint Martins in 2001 and worked in Tokyo for a year. After declining jobs at Yohji Yamamoto, they decided to return to the UK and launch Swash. They showcased their first collection at the Festival International des Arts de la Mode in Hyères in 2004, where they won the Fashion Grand Prix and were awarded a further two prizes.

Swash___*91/100*

Collaboration is integral to the label's success. In 2005 *Swash* reworked the Absolut Vodka logo into a bra T-shirt. As part of their Spring/Summer 05 collection, they produced a short video that was shown on the infamous art and fashion website SHOWstudio, founded by Nick Knight. For Spring/Summer 06, *Swash* worked on a short film with Johnny Barrington, who has produced music videos for artists such as Mylo and Belle and Sebastian.

Swash designs experiment with the idea of multifunctional shape and print. They are interested in how a garment can be interchangeable: a bag that becomes a coat, a coat that can accommodate three people. Contradictions are also important, for example, how the luxurious becomes the obscene, how seriousness becomes laughable and how beauty can be bizarre.

Shapes in their basic form are always inspirational to the team. 'The way these shapes can be manipulated and worked into something desirable and intriguing. Shapes are the building blocks of an interesting pattern. The cut, the fit, all transpire from an understanding of shape and geometry.'

The designers don't like to define their boundaries too strongly. Like their design philosophy, their designs are intended to appeal to a whole array of different people for different reasons. 'The ideal is that people buy our clothes for different reasons and that each particular garment means something different to each person.'

www.swash.co.uk

1. Printed Boston-bag jacket, S/S 06. **2.** Bike cape and printed trousers, A/W 04. **3.** Cotton jacket embellished with appliquéd 'eye' motifs, S/S 06. **4–5.** Parachute jacket; printed chute top. S/S 06. **6–9.** Candy jacquard blouse; triangle jacquard 'jacksack' and puff skirt; square shoulder top; printed dungarees. S/S 07.

3

4

5

7

*'The cut, the fit, all transpire from an understanding of shape and geometry'*____**Swash**

8

9

Born to Liberian parents in New York, Telfar Clemens relocated to Liberia with his mother and four siblings at the age of five, and returned to the US when civil war broke out in his parents' native country. Working in New York as a DJ, model and fashion designer, in 2003 he created his own collection by deconstructing and reconstructing vintage clothing, selling his garments in New York City's Lower East Side and SoHo boutiques. In 2004 he went to college to study for a business degree and then launched his own fashion label, Telfar.

Telfar___*92/100*

Designing practical and functional clothes is Clemens's aim. As he describes it, he creates clothing according to 'what is needed'. Defining contemporary fashion as 'funny and predictable at certain times', Clemens believes that he is personally innovative by 'designing for future needs' using an unrestricted aesthetic.

Bringing originality and thought to his designs, Clemens creates unisex collections for 'smart' customers based on the principles of comfortable street fashion and artistic complexity. His multi-functional garments can usually be worn in two ways, depending on the wearer's gender, and key pieces include jodpur-like wrap pants, hooded double-sleeved turtlenecks and garments with bubble silhouettes that are suited to both the male and female form.

Utilizing wearable, relaxed fabrics such as cotton jersey in neutral palettes of grey, black, white and taupe, the label succeeds in its quest to create easy pieces with an edgy urban vibe.

www.telfar.net

1. Burlap dress, sun hat and flask necklace, S/S 08. 2. White hooded jacket and jeans, 2005. 3. Felt trench bomber and skinny pants, S/S 07. 4–7. Black felt jacket; bubble t-shirt (can be turned upside-down and worn as shorts); cotton fleece (shirt doubles as a scarf); uni-strap jumper and hat/scarf/glove combination. A/W 07. 8. Nylon top and neoprene shorts, S/S 08. 9. Felt trench bomber and skinny pants, S/S 07.

3

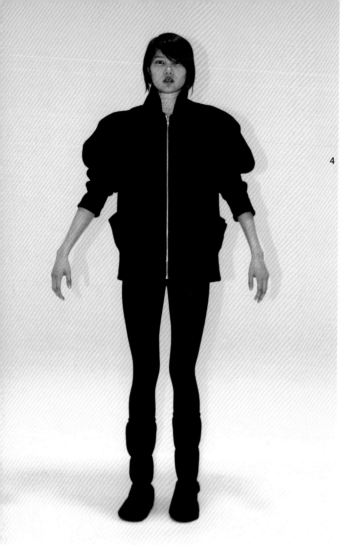

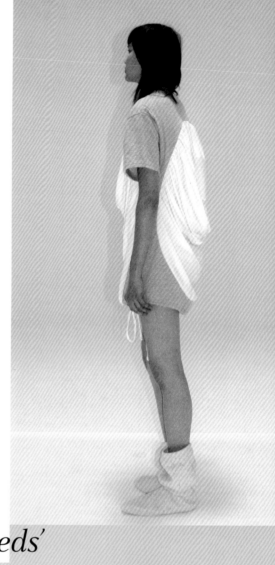

4

'Designing for future needs'
___Te__r

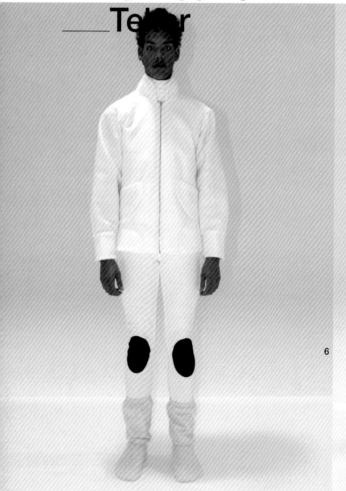

6

8

9

1

Tillmann Lauterbach was born in Germany but raised in Ibiza. In 2000, after working for Deutsche Bank for two years, he finally realized that fashion was his calling. He enrolled at ESMOD in Paris, graduating in 2003 with a diploma in fashion design and pattern-cutting. He worked for Plein Sud in Paris before launching his own label in 2005.

Tillmann Lauterbach

___93/100

The designer's philosophy is to create silent collections, which are understatements made of the finest fabrics. 'The people who buy my collections don't buy to show off a name or intimidate others by opulence. These people buy the clothes for themselves as a special, unique garment.'

Contrasts are key to Lauterbach as he explores the rawness of cloth. 'I see fashion like writing or music. My aim is to convey the maximum using the fewest words possible. A good design should work like good music when it's not played at full volume. I am obsessed with purifying my lines; minimalism on a complex level maybe.' The designer's collections are inspired by abstract thoughts or feelings. 'I choose this open ground on purpose to tell my stories, always trying to reveal the hidden beauty of things.'

Lauterbach's design process involves him being a spectator of ordinary life. 'I watch people and my surroundings. A gesture, a stone, a sound happening in the right moment of time can trigger a bigger picture. I collect these pictures in my head until they assemble into some sort of story or emotion that I find fitting to the time and state of mind we are living in.' He then chooses fabrics and researches different processes to refine them. Alongside this, he defines a colour palette that suits the emotion and flow of the collection. Then comes the volume and finishing.

'I honestly don't try to set trends or be modern,' explains Lauterbach. 'Being the person I am, living here and now, aware of my senses, I think it would be impossible to create a collection that is not related to the present.'

www.tillmannlauterbach.com

1–2. Asymmetric pleated silk dress; cotton playsuit. 'DEPARTURE ff/OUR', S/S 07. 3. Research photo for 'S/pain', S/S 06. 4. Sheer top, S/S 08. 5. Wool knitted dress, 'INSANE/out', A/W 07. 6. Study on garments and pleats, 2005. 7. Personal project, 'Decline', 2006.

3

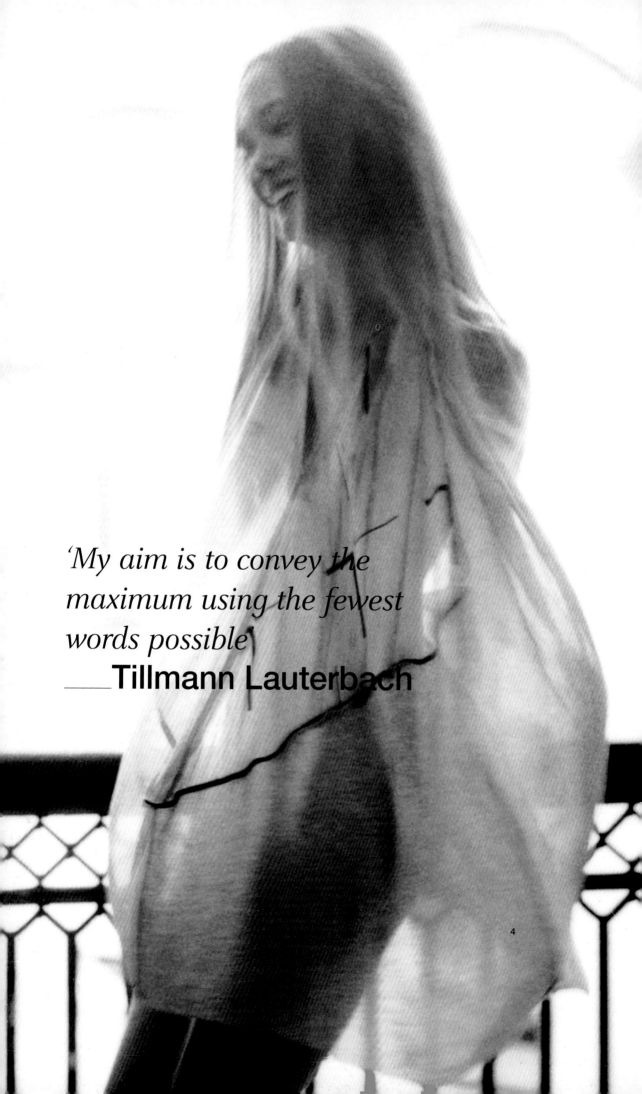

'My aim is to convey the maximum using the fewest words possible'
____Tillmann Lauterbach

4

5

6

7

Based in the USA, Tim Hamilton launched his menswear collection in 2007. With a background in luxury design, Hamilton had previously worked at Ralph Lauren and J. Crew. He decided to follow his dream and launch his own signature collection after recognizing a void in the men's market for luxury sportswear. In 2007 the Council of Fashion Designers of America (CFDA) nominated Hamilton for the Swarovski Award for Menswear, which honours emerging newcomers on the fashion scene.

Tim Hamilton___*94/100*

Describe your design philosophy. *High-end modern menswear fashion with a speciality feel, well-executed designs and high standards of production that has highly controlled distribution in global boutiques.*

How would you define your aesthetic? *Modern, clean and minimal. It incorporates different takes on menswear archetypes and is inspired by travelling. It is streetwear style meets with splendour.*

What is the most enjoyable part of design? *The actual design process – coming up with concepts, finding beautiful fabrics and yarns. Actually creating something that is being bought and worn is still an inconceivable idea in my head; it's quite flattering.*

How would you describe your customer? *I would say he knows fashion well, but I also attract guys who don't. He is someone who appreciates quality, longevity and good design. He thinks of it more as an investment.*

How would you describe your creative process? *It honestly changes from season to season. I am inspired by what I read or see. I'm very visual. I react to a lot of bold colours and people who take risks with confidence. After the initial inspiration kicks in for the season, I usually think of the one thing that moves as a bigger group. Then I start with the fabric design and colour, then drop the bodies into the fabrics and go from there with the proportions, etc.*

How would you define contemporary fashion? *In its current state it seems that there is a new wave of menswear designer, but honestly the only fresh things I see come out of Europe or Japan.*

Who or what informs your work? *Art, politics, the change of season, my friends and travels.*

www.tim-hamilton.com

1. Shirts and sweaters, 'Resort' collection for Bergdorf Goodman, 2008. **2–6.** Anorak with zip detail; double-breasted trench and trousers; grey suit jacket and cotton trousers; striped blazer and jeans; PVC jacket and shorts. All S/S 08. **7–8.** Striped collarless shirt; roundneck sweater and jeans. 'Resort' collection, 2008.

2

3

5

6

'*Modern, clean and minimal*'
___Tim Hamilton

7

8

Canadian Todd Lynn graduated from Ryerson University in Toronto in 1991 and worked for several Canadian fashion designers as a technical adviser. From 1996 he designed for rock bands and performers, including U2, Marilyn Manson, PJ Harvey, Mick Jagger and The Rolling Stones. He went on to study at Central Saint Martins in London, graduating in 2000 and becoming the right-hand man of London-based designer Roland Mouret. He launched his own label in 2006.

Todd Lynn___*95/100*

Lynn's clothes are androgynous and inspired by his rock and roll experiences. He explains, 'My first foray into this industry came courtesy of my bespoke work for the élite of the music world. I have been able to provide something extra that they need. It's that exclusivity where they get a one-off piece made especially for them.' Lynn's work attracted female admirers who saw the bespoke pieces he had created for male celebrities and wanted something similar. As a result he developed menswear that was tailored to fit women too, producing men's styles, then reducing the size and reconfiguring them to fit a woman's body. 'There has always been a blurring of the line between masculine and feminine in my work,' says Lynn, 'and rock stars have been blurring those lines for a long time.' Tailoring for both men and women, Lynn creates a distinctive long, lean and sharp silhouette that is thoroughly modern.

'Anything can trigger an idea,' believes Lynn, but he admits that he finds it a challenge to work in an industry where his vision is held up to such scrutiny. 'It's all about knowing how far to push and how much to hold back. I take influences from the past and combine them with a modern edge to push ideas into new territory.'

A minimalist approach to colour characterizes Lynn's edgy and dark rock-and-roll cool. By incorporating traditional tailoring and contemporary deconstruction, his collections straddle the music and fashion worlds. As he explains, 'It's all about making the person feel like a star and putting them at the centre of attention the moment they walk into a room.'

www.toddlynn.com

1. Short suit and shirt, photoshoot for *10* magazine, S/S 07. 2. Background image from Todd Lynn's web site. 3–6. White suit with buttoned vest; cream jacket with bow; sleeveless shirt with loose pants; pinstripe suit. All S/S 07. 7. Suit jacket with cotton shirt, A/W 07. 8. Artwork, A/W 08.

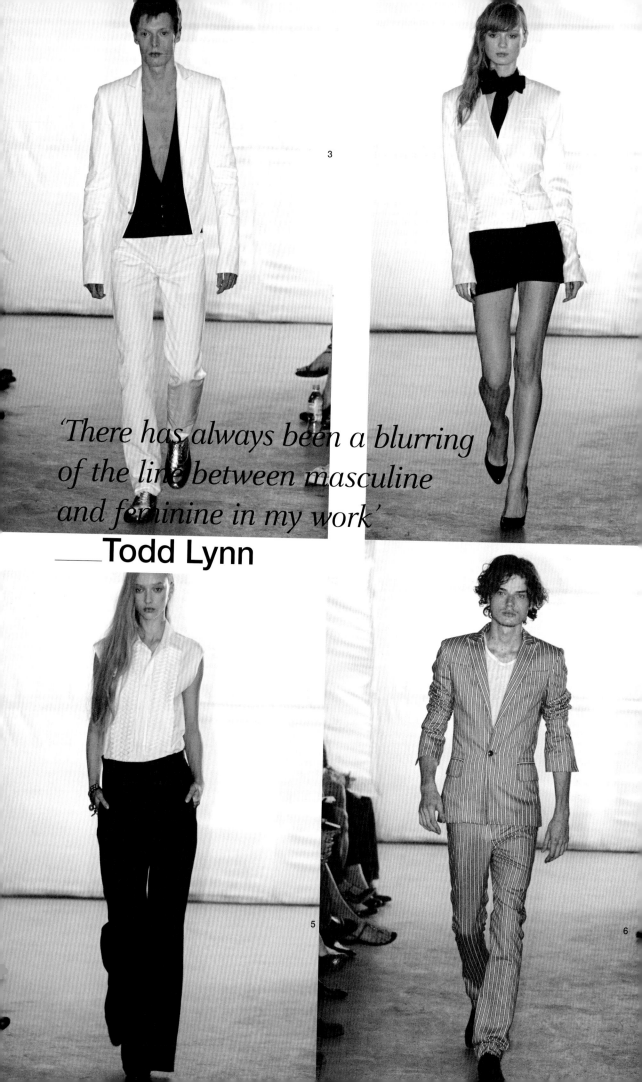

3

'There has always been a blurring
of the line between masculine
and feminine in my work'
____Todd Lynn

5

6

7

8

'I prefer my ideas to evolve naturally. I don't believe that newness can be achieved by just turning down your previous point of view on a six-month basis,' affirms Buenos Aires-born designer Jessica Trosman. Still based in South America, Trosman shows her collections in Paris twice a year.

Trosman___*96/100*

Trosman originally studied fashion design at the University of Miami, before returning to Argentina to work as a consultant for fashion labels. She launched her own collection in 2002, and her work is characterized by a fusion of different materials such as feathers, plants and paint in her garments.

Designers such as Charles Eames and Frank Lloyd Wright inspire *Trosman*. She attempts to use architecture as the concept behind her collections, distancing herself from the idea of being a fashion designer. Trosman attests that it is not her intention to work aesthetically. 'I just work with my tools, my knowledge, my lack of knowledge – all of this turns into something.'

Describing her creative process as being about persistence, Trosman states, 'It's just regular hard work. I can't remember the exact time or the exact thing that inspired me or when I came up with a vision. I just take some big decisions every day.'

According to Trosman, the most challenging aspect of design is finding the chemistry of materials, the fluidity of shapes, the weight and the finishes. 'I don't have a very solid opinion. I am not a fashion specialist. I try to come up with new ideas but I am certainly not affecting contemporary fashion. I always try to evolve from my previous work – that is what makes the whole process essentially innovative.'

www.trosman.com

1. Beaded viscose necklace, A/W 06. 2. Fine-knit sleeveless top, S/S 08. 3. Printed wool sweater, A/W 06. 4. Wool sweater with cotton pants, A/W 06. 5. Draped sweater and pants with pocket detail, A/W 07. 6. Beaded scarf, S/S 08. 7. Silk dress, S/S 08. 8. Silk jacket, S/S 08.

2

6

8

7

'*I prefer my ideas to evolve naturally*'___**Trosman**

1

2

3

Barcelona native Txell Miras not only has her own women's collection, but she is also responsible for designing Neil Barrett's womenswear line. After graduating from the Milan Domus Academy in 1999, she was employed by Barrett, who motivated her to develop her own label. In 2003 she presented her debut collection on the catwalk of Gaudí Fashion Week in Barcelona.

Txell Miras___*97/100*

Describe your design philosophy. *My design philosophy lies between formal body works and conceptual art. In fashion I'm interested in investigating shapes and patterns with a hard conceptual background.*

How would you define your aesthetic? *Hard and dark with a touch of nostalgia.*

What is the most enjoyable part of design? *Thinking about the concept and the first part of the experimentation process with the fabrics and patterns. I also like to make the looks for the show.*

How would you describe your customer? *Women who are interested in design. As I'm not a well-known designer my pieces are bought by women who have an interest in garment shapes; those who look for different clothes.*

How would you describe your creative process? *Work and more work. First of all I develop an abstract concept that comes from my background. Then I start working with my hands, old patterns and fabrics.*

Who or what informs your work? *I'm very interested in cinema, literature, art and music. I'm normally inspired by all these things together. Every life or cultural experience you have feeds your brain, and while you work your brain generates the connections to create new ideas. I admire the work of such people as Marcel Duchamp, Christian Boltanski, Joseph Beuys, Witold Gombrowicz, Franz Kafka, Roberto Bolaño, Andrei Tarkovsky, Carl Dreyer and many others.*

What is the most challenging aspect of design? *To survive in the market with your own style. To remain independent.*

www.txellmiras.eu

1. Volume dress, 'Biography of Biographies', S/S 05. 2–3. One-shoulder top with pleated skirt and leggings; top and skirt. 'Persona', S/S 04, inspired by Ingmar Bergman's film of the same name. 4. Poster artwork, 2006. 5. Leather jacket with old photographs, inspired by the works of Christian Boltansky, pre-collection work, 2003. 6. Dress for Mango Fashion Awards, S/S 08. 7. Patchwork top and skirt inspired by the 'arte povera' movement, pre-collection work, 2002. 8. 'Descorsetant' show, S/S 07. 9. Book bag, 2003.

4

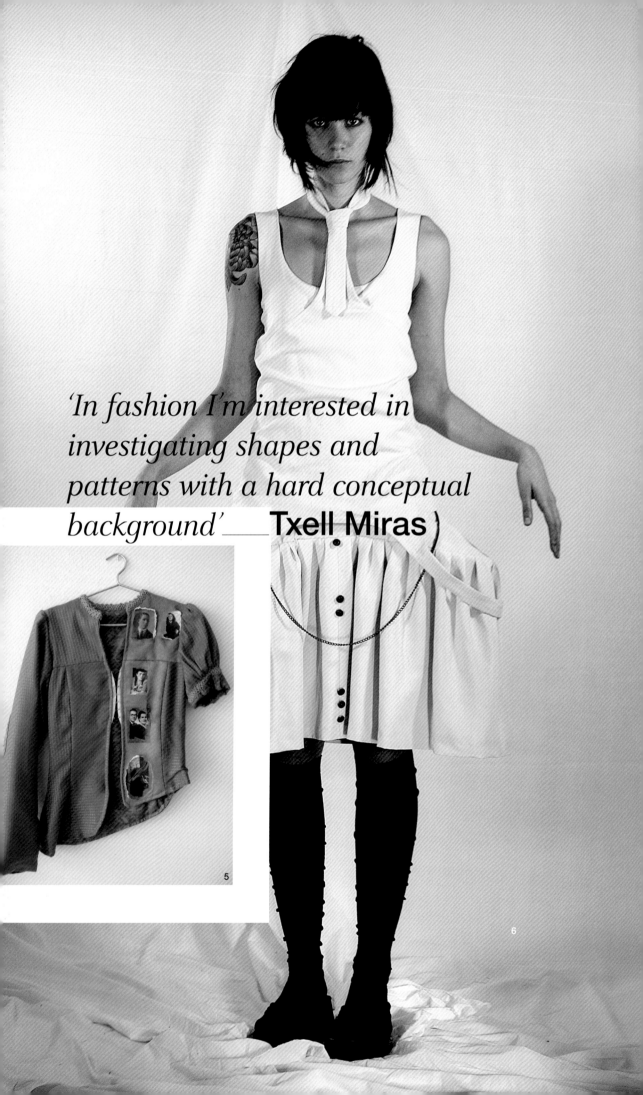

*'In fashion I'm interested in investigating shapes and patterns with a hard conceptual background'*___**Txell Miras**

5

6

7

8

9

Designed by Philip Stephens, Unconditional was launched in 2003 as a collection of luxury menswear for his fashion boutique, the Concrete Shop London. The line had immediate success, and in 2005 a womenswear collection was introduced. The label was invited to show its Autumn/Winter 06/07 collection on-schedule at London Fashion Week, following a small off-schedule show of the Spring/Summer 06 line.

Unconditional___*98/100*

Describe your design philosophy. *To create interesting, wearable, desirable clothes. I very much like clothes not to take over their wearer – so fairly simple and clean garments that maybe help project the person inside, nothing over-designed.*

How would you define your aesthetic? *Often a marriage and combination of polar opposites. Mixing the formal with the informal, the sexy with the understated and the simple with the more complex. I think* Unconditional *mixes my very British background with a more rebellious streak.*

What is the most enjoyable part of design? *I guess seeing someone look great in what you've designed.*

How would you describe your customer? *Really varied, but I guess they all tend to be interested in fashion and design without being slaves to it. They want something a bit individual without wanting to look like a freak or a fashion victim.*

How would you describe your creative process? *Lots of things can inspire me so it's truly a varied process. And it's often a challenge in terms of trying to marry or edit seemingly disparate influences and ideas.*

How would you define contemporary fashion? *It is now totally varied and anything goes. There are so many 'trends' at once, and that's a really good thing. So I think contemporary fashion is about investing in quality that is going to look and feel good and in simply wearing pieces that suit you as an individual.*

Who or what informs your work? *Strangely I find it is most often things deep in my subconscious, but without question nature is the one constant that always inspires and amazes me and is most locked in my subconscious. From its colours to its textures and shapes.*

www.unconditional.uk.com

1–4. PVC puff-sleeve coat; shrunken sheepskin jacket with fine-jersey top; cotton basketweave top; zipped leather bomber with printed t-shirt and denim jeans with zip piping. All A/W 07. **5.** Catwalk show, S/S 08.

5

Austrian Ute Ploier graduated from the University of Applied Arts Vienna in 2003 and was awarded the menswear award at the Festival International des Arts de la Mode in Hyères. In 2004 she debuted her Autumn/Winter 04/05 collection at Paris Men's Fashion Week.

Ute Ploier___99/100

Describe your design philosophy. *I am a woman designing menswear. I decided to do so because my work is about investigating roles, codes and images in our society. I felt I should reverse the common image of a fashion designer, which still very often means a man designing clothes for women. My design philosophy is to subtly push the boundaries in men's fashion, but at the same time to respect the needs of the person who will wear my designs.*

How would you define your aesthetic? *Clear, logical but with surreal or fantastic elements.*

What is the most enjoyable part of design? *There are many aspects in the design process that I enjoy: the search for the theme of the collection; researching collection material; finding a solution for a complex detail; and the moment when everything comes together and falls into place.*

How would you describe your customer? *He appreciates solutions that go beyond traditional menswear without neglecting its roots.*

How would you describe your creative process? *For me, it's about developing a concept or story and translating it into all the parts that form a collection – the fabrics, silhouettes, details, etc.*

How would you define contemporary fashion? *Contemporary is what is relevant at the moment. There is no timeline for contemporary fashion. A suit from 1900 can be as contemporary as a worker's overall or a piece from a S/S 08 collection.*

What is the most challenging aspect of design? *To constantly ask questions, and to be able to take a step back, rethink and maybe alter decisions you have made.*

How are you personally innovative in fashion design? *My collections are not about constantly promoting a certain look or a social group. They are about the diversity of images or roleplays in our society. Fashion is about change. I try to find new strategies or crafts for every collection.*

www.uteploier.com

1–3. Leather jacket, knitted sweater and hat with metal pin; checked loden shirt and longsleeved printed t-shirt. 'Pioneers', A/W 05. **4–7.** Cotton trousers and printed jacket; leather jacket, stonewashed trousers and cotton hat; waxed cotton trench and trousers with printed tanktop and hat; stonewashed parka, knitted sweater and cotton trousers. All A/W 05. **8.** Striped shirt, cotton-metal blend suit and handpainted striped bag, 'Charming Crooks Transglobal World Tour', S/S 06. **9.** Satin bomber with epaulets made from antique buttons, handpainted striped trousers. Handpainted black and gold sweater with enzyme-washed linen blazer. Both S/S 06. **10.** Horizontal pinstripe suit with nylon shirt, 'Time-Loopers', S/S 08.

4

'Clear, logical but with surreal
or fantastic elements'
___Ute Ploier

6

7

8

9

10

BE.YOU*(K)

1

2

3

Japanese-born Yuko Yoshitake studied menswear at the London
College of Fashion. She won Best Menswear and Collection of the
Year awards at the 2003 Graduate Fashion Week in London. Her
collection, a hybrid of luxury streetwear and classic tailoring, was
sold to Topman, who produced the designs under her own-name
label. Yoshitake worked for fashion designer Peter Jensen before
setting up her own label in London with the support of the Centre
for Fashion Enterprise.

Yuko Yoshitake____*100/100*

Yoshitake is described as a 'hands-on' designer. 'I try to be true to myself. Clothes should
reflect my personality. I attempt to communicate something through the clothes, to
make people think or feel something.'

Her collections are aimed at the top end of the menswear market, and manipulate the
silhouettes and fabrics of traditional tailoring to create a style that is relaxed and
playful. 'I'm drawn to domestic, everyday objects and I very much like the idea of
making the ordinary a little bit extraordinary. I don't really use sharp lines, and I
prefer a slightly rounded look, which is maybe interesting as my designs are actually
quite masculine.'

Classic English tailoring and vintage sportswear influence Yoshitake. The quality of
the cut and unexpected detailing are very important to her. People in the street often
inspire her. 'I did a knitted cuff for jackets and coats that looked like a jumper poking
out from the sleeve. An old man I saw on a bus whose coat was too short was responsible
for that. I quite like eccentric people, maybe unfashionable people and old people. I'm
not really inspired by fame or celebrity.'

According to Yoshitake, there are too many cheap, throwaway clothes available today.
'Clothes should last and not be for one season. Environmentally that is an important
issue, but also it's about caring for something and appreciating it for what it is. There
is a part of contemporary fashion that encourages waste. I like timeless things so I
often use recycled clothes as I like the history they already have in them.'

www.yukoyoshitake.com

1. Cotton trousers with knee pads and panel vest, S/S 05. **2.** Wool jacket with cotton t-shirt and jeans, S/S 08. **3.** Double-
zip wool cardigan, vest shirt and cummerbund-waisted wool trousers, A/W 07. **4.** Spectacle-print artwork, S/S 07.
5. Dinner setting-print artwork, S/S 07. **6–7.** Baseball t-shirt, hooded gabardine jacket and padded-knee denim jeans;
pinstripe cotton 'nurse' dress with merino wool shrug. All S/S 06. **8.** Cotton waistcoat with vintage buttons, classic bib
shirt and pleated cotton skirt, S/S 07. **9.** Meat-print cotton hoody, A/W 05.

5

6

7

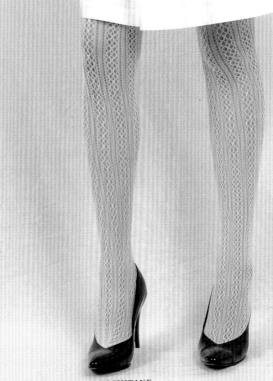

9

'*Clothes should last and not be for one season*'
___**Yuko Yoshitake**

8

Designer Contacts

*****L____www.cinqetoilesluxe.com
6 ⁷/₈ (Six and Seven Eighths)____www.antoniociutto.co.uk
0044____www.0044paris.com
Aimee McWilliams____www.aimeemcwilliams.com
Aitor Throup____www.aitorthroup.com
Aleksandra Olenska____www.aleksandraolenska.com
Alena Akhmadullina____www.alenaakhmadullina.com
Alice McCall____www.alicemccall.com
Aminaka Wilmont____www.aminakawilmont.com
Antoine Peters____www.antoinepeters.com
Apostolos Mitropoulos____www.apostolosm.com
Ashish____www.ashish.co.uk
Avsh Alom Gur____www.avshalomgur.com
Basso & Brooke____www.bassoandbrooke.com
Bo Van Melskens____www.bovanmelskens.com
Bora Aksu____www.boraaksu.com
Borba Margo____borbamargo@gmail.com
C. Neeon____www.cneeon.de
Carola Euler____www.carolaeuler.com
Cassette Playa____www.cassetteplaya.com
Cathy Pill____www.cathypill.com
Cecilia Sörenson____www.ceciliasorensen.com
Chris Liu____www.chrisliulondon.com
Christoph Fröhlich____www.christophfroehlich.de
Commuun____www.commuun.com
Customers Own Property____www.customersownproperty.com
Danielle Scutt____www.daniellescutt.com
Denis Simachëv____www.denissimachev.com
Deryck Walker____www.deryckwalker.com
Duckie Brown____www.duckiebrown.com
El Delgado Buil____www.eldelgadobuil.com
Emilio de la Morena____www.emiliodelamorena.com
Erdem____www.erdem.co.uk
Eric Lebon____www.ericlebon.com
Felder Felder____www.felderfelder.com
Felipe Oliveira Baptista____www.felipeoliveirabaptista.com
Finsk____www.finsk.com
Frank Leder____www.frank-leder.com
Gardem____www.gardem.net
Gavin Douglas____www.gavindouglasfashion.com
Hall Ohara____www.hallohara.com
Haltbar____www.haltbar.de
Hamish Morrow____www.hamishmorrow.com
Heather Blake____www.heatherblake.co.uk
Henrik Vibskov____www.henrikvibskov.com
Horace____www.myspace.com/horace_tv
Ioannis Dimitrousis____www.ioannisdimitrousis.com
Jain Close/Marc Szwajcer____www.jcms.be
Jantaminiau____www.jantaminiau.com
Jean-Pierre Braganza____www.jeanpierrebraganza.com

Jens Laugesen___*www.jenslaugesen.com*
Jolibe___*www.jolibe.com*
Jonathan Saunders___*www.jonathan-saunders.com*
Katarzyna Szczotarska___*www.katarzynaszczotarska.com*
Kosmetique Label___*www.kosmetiquelabel.com*
Laitinen___*www.agenturv.de*
Louis de Gama___*www.louisdegama.com*
Louise Amstrup___*www.louise-amstrup.com*
Lutz___*POLUX 81 Rue du Temple 75003 Paris*
Manish Arora___*www.manisharora.ws*
Meadham/Kirchhoff___*www.meadhamkirchhoff.com*
Miki Fukai___*www.mikifukai.com*
Mikio Sakabe___*www.mikiosakabe.com*
Modernist___*www.modernistonline.com*
Nasir Mazhar___*+44 (0)20 7729 2770*
Natalia Brilli___*www.nataliabrilli.fr*
Nathan Jenden___*www.nathanjenden.com*
Olanic___*www.olanic.co.uk*
Osman Yousefzada___*www.osmanyousefzada.com*
Patrik Söderstam___*www.patriksoderstam.com*
Pelican Avenue___*www.pelicanavenue.com*
Petar Petrov___*www.petarpetrov.com*
Peter Bertsch___*+32 495 133 060*
Peter Pilotto___*www.peterpilotto.com*
Postweiler Hauber___*www.postweilerhauber.com*
PPQ___*www.ppqclothing.com*
Pulver___*www.pulver-studio.de*
Rad Hourani___*www.radhourani.com*
Raeburn Design___*www.raeburndesign.co.uk*
Richard Nicoll___*www.richardnicoll.com*
Robert Normand___*www.robertnormand.com*
Romina Karamanea___*www.rominakaramanea.com*
Romy Smits___*www.romysmits.com*
Rubecksen Yamanaka___*www.rubecksenyamanaka.com*
Seïko Taki___*www.seiko-taki-paris.com*
Siv Støldal___*www.odd.at*
Slobodan Mihajlovic___*www.myspace.com/slobodanmihajlovic*
Slow and Steady Wins the Race___*www.slowandsteadywinstherace.com*
Spijkers en Spijkers___*www.spijkersenspijkers.com*
Steve J & Yoni P___*www.stevejandyonip.com*
Swash___*www.swash.co.uk*
Telfar___*www.telfar.net*
Tillmann Lauterbach___*www.tillmannlauterbach.com*
Tim Hamilton___*www.tim-hamilton.com*
Todd Lynn___*www.toddlynn.com*
Trosman___*www.trosman.com*
Txell Miras___*www.txellmiras.eu*
Unconditional___*www.unconditional.uk.com*
Ute Ploier___*www.uteploier.com*
Yuko Yoshitake___*www.yukoyoshitake.com*

Picture Credits

The author and publisher would like to thank the following institutions and individuals for providing photographic images for use in this book. In all cases, every effort has been made to credit the copyright holders, but should there be any omissions or errors the publisher would be pleased to insert the appropriate acknowledgement in any subsequent edition of this book.

Front cover: Dress by Erdem; photography Lancton; styling Claire Durbridge; hair Juan Carlos @ One Makeup; makeup Claudine Henderson @ Naked Artists; model Alina @ Take2 — *******L 1:** Photography *****L. **2 & 8:** Photography Alex Klesta. **3, 7 & 9:** Photography Ari Versluis & Ellie Uyttenbroeck. **4 & 6:** Photography Filipe da Rocha — **6 7/8 1:** Photography David Jones/fuk.co.uk. **2:** Photography Mitchel Sams. **3:** Photography David Wojtowycz/Antonio Ciutto — **0044 1, 5–8 & 11:** Photography Ami Matsumura. **2 & 9:** Photography Taka Mayumi. **4:** Photography Andreas Licht. **10:** Photography Yannick Coupannec — **Aimee McWilliams 1, 2 & 5:** Photography David Cernuschi; styling Aimee McWilliams; hair Kenna@eramanagement.com; makeup Adam di Cruz; model Stefie Du Monceau — **Aitor Throup 1–3:** Photography Jez Tozer. **4:** Photography Jez Tozer for i-D magazine; styling Mark McMahon. **7–10:** Photography Ross Williams. **11–12:** Photography Jez Tozer; styling Stephen Mann; animation Daniel Gill & Anna Sheldon. **13:** Photography courtesy of ITS#5 — **Aleksandra Olenska 1:** Photography Rob Wyatt for 10 magazine; styling Lucy Ewing. **2–5:** Photography Dennis Schoenberg — **Alena Akhmadullina 1–6:** Photography Dan & Corina Lecca. **7:** Photography Sakharov Igor — **Alice McCall 1, 3, 5, 6 & 8–10:** Photography Pierre Toussaint. **2 & 7:** Photography Paul Empson; model Simone Kerr — **Aminaka Wilmont 1 & 6:** Photography Karin Gunnarsson. **2:** Photography Karin Gunnarsson; hair Kizi; makeup Meagan Chau; model Brooke. **4:** Photography Karin Gunnarsson; hair & makeup Vickie Ellis; model Yasser. **5, 7 & 8:** Photography Karin Gunnarsson; hair & makeup Vickie Ellis; model Cathy — **Antoine Peters 1 & 2:** Photography Jochem Sanders. **4 & 5:** Photography Peter Stigter. **6:** Photography Antoine Peters; graphic design Karen van de Kraats. **7:** Photography & design Karen van de Kraats — **Apostolos Mitropoulos 1, 2 & 4–9:** Photography John Mitropoulos; hair & makeup Stellar. **3:** Photography George Kalfamanolis; hair & makeup Eleftheria Savopoulou — **Ashish 1, 2 & 8:** Photography Will Sanders; hair Tom Kembery; makeup Shama @ CLM; model Nadja B @ FM Models. **3:** Photography Will Sanders. **4:** Photography Will Sanders; hair Tom Kembery; makeup Shama @ CLM; model Aisha @ FM Models. **5 & 6:** Photography Leigh Keily; styling Karen Binns. **7:** Photography catwalking.com; styling Celestine Cooney — **Avsh Alom Gur 1:** Photography Avsh Alom Gur. **2:** Photography Vanessa Ellis; styling Hannah Bhuiya. **3:** Photography Vanessa Ellis; styling Oonagh O'Hagan — **Basso & Brooke 1 & 4:** Photography catwalking.com. **2 & 7:** Photography Fernanda Calfat — **Bo Van Melskens** All photographs Christian Weigel — **Bora Aksu 2:** Photography Mark Sanders; styling Alison Elwin; model: Alina Levichkina @ Take2. All other photographs Ian Gillet; illustrations Bora Aksu — **Borba Margo 1, 3, 5 & 7:** Photography Tara Khan. **2, 4 & 6:** Photography Gustavo Camilo — **C. Neeon 5:** Photography Shoji Fujii. All other photographs c.neeon — **Carola Euler 2, 3 & 6:** Photography Aitken Jolly; model Sean Bourke @ Independent Talent. All other photographs Carola Euler — **Cassette Playa 1:** Video still by CMYK Hole (Jo Apps, Zephyre & Thomas Whitehead); model Tomoya @ Pineal Eye. **2:** Photography catwalking.com; model Johan @ Premier. **3–4:** Photography catwalking.com — **Cathy Pill 1–4 & 7:** Photography Gregory Derkenne. **5 & 8:** Photography Etienne Tordoire. **6:** Photography Raf Thienpont — **Cecilia Sörensen 1, 3, 5, 7 & 8:** Photography Nacho Alegre; styling Johanna Ahlberg. **2 & 6:** Photography Lina Persson; styling Johanna Ahlberg. **4, 9 & 10:** Photography Roope Alho — **Chris Liu 1 & 3–9:** Photography Fabrice Lachant; styling Britta Burger. **2:** Photography Fabrice Lachant; styling Lucy Ewing — **Christoph Fröhlich 1 & 6–9:** Photography Etienne Tordoir. **2–4:** Photography Florian Schwarz; concept & styling studio format-c. **5 & 10:** Photography Stefano Guindani; concept, studio format-c — **Commuun 1:** Photography Carole Peyrot. **2–4:** Photography Lukas Wassmann. All styling Sohei Yoshida — **Customers Own Property 1 & 5:** Photography Joachim Müller-Ruchholtz. **2 & 4:** Photography Sabine Bräuninger. **3:** Photography Robin Bale. **7:** Photography Kim Weston-Arnold — **Danielle Scutt** All photography catwalking.com — **Denis Simachëv 1, 3 & 6:** Photography Ivan Makarov. **7 & 8:** Photography Dmitry Livshiz — **Deryck Walker 1, 2, 4 & 6–10:** Photography Andrea Cellerino. **3:** Photography Paul Moore. **5:** Photography Deryck Walker — **Duckie Brown** All photography Platon — **El Delgado Buil 1:** Photograph courtesy of Circuit; model Manuel Polo. **2:** Photography Bielsol. **3–4:** Photograph courtesy of Circuit. **5:** Photography Bielsol; model Octave. **6:** Photography Ico Mateo. **7:** Photography Ico Mateo; model Manuel Polo — **Emilio de la Morena 1:** Photography Marc Regas; styling Sarah Richardson. **2, 5 & 6:** Photography Mari Sarai; styling Raquel Garcia. **4:** Photography Marc Regas — **Erdem** All photography catwalking.com; styling Samantha Willoughby — **Eric Lebon 1–3, 7 & 10:** Photography Jeremy. **4:** Photography Wiglius de Bie; styling Gregory Delos. **5:** Photography Stephane Coedel. **6–9:** Photography Shoji Fujii — **Felder Felder 1 & 8:** Photography Simian Coates; styling Grace Woodward; hair James Rowe. **2 & 9:** Photography Wendy Bevan; styling Grace Woodward; makeup Georgina Graham. **4–7:** Photography Adrian Wilson; styling Grace Woodward; makeup Andrew Gallimore — **Felipe Oliveira Baptista 1 & 6:** Photography Felipe Oliveira Baptista. **2–5:** Photography Etienne Tordoir — **Finsk 1:** Photography Jason Jameson. **2:** Photography Aleksi Niemela. **3 & 4:** Photography Finsk. **5 & 6:** Photography Max Oppenheim. **7 & 8:** Animation Jason Jameson — **Frank Leder** All photography Gregor Hohenberg — **Gardem 1:** Photography Andrew Laam. **2 & 8:** Photography James Mason; styling Antonio Salgado. **3–6:** Photography Camille Viver; styling Alex Aikiu. **7:** Photography Roger Moukarzel; styling Garen Demerdjin — **Gavin Douglas 1–3:** Photography Ian Gillet; styling Karen Binns; hair L'oréal Paris — **Hall Ohara 1, 2, 4 & 5:** Photography Kyoko Homma. **6–9:** Photography Yasumasa Yonehara; hair & makeup Yoshikazu; model Chiaki Kuriyama — **Haltbar 1:** Photography Seeberger.Buss. **2, 3 & 5–8:** Photography Markus Jans. **4 & 9:** Photography Thomas Degen. **10:** Photography Judith Buss — **Hamish Morrow 1 & 3:** Photography Warren Du Preez/Nick Thornton-Jones; hair Dejan Cekanovic; makeup Tania Chianale. **2:** Photography Warren Du Preez/Nick Thornton-Jones; styling George Cortina; hair Eugene Souleiman; makeup Aaron deMay. **4–7:** Photography Warren Du Preez/Nick Thornton-Jones; styling Suzanne Lee; hair Rafael Salley; makeup Tania Chianale. **8:** Photography Stefan Zeisler; styling Michelle Duguid; hair Christian Wood; makeup Tania Chianale. **9:** Photography Warren Du Preez/Nick Thornton-Jones; hair & makeup Wendy Rowe; digital projection by United Visual Artists — **Heather Blake** All photography Akio — **Henrik Vibskov** All photography the company of Henrik Vibskov — **Horace 1, 3 & 5:** Photography Adam Entwisle; model Mark Roe. **2:** Photography Adam Entwisle; model Jessie Hill. **4 & 7:** Photography Magnus Hastings; model Andrew @ Pineal Eye. **6:** Photography Magnus Hastings; model Ella @ Pineal Eye — **Ioannis Dimitrousis 1 & 4:** Photography Dimitris Theocharis. **2 & 5:** Photography Panos Davios. **3:** Photography Ionnis Dimitrousis. **6:** Photography Nana Varveropoulou — **Jain Close/Marc Szwajcer 1 & 6–9:** Video Marc Szwajcer; styling Jain Close; model Helene Petit. **2, 3 & 6:** Photography Marc Szwajcer; model Jain Close — **Jantaminiau 1 & 3–6:** Photography Wiglius de Bie. **2:** Photography Alique. **7:** Photography Fritz Kok — **Jean-Pierre Braganza 1:** Photography Richard Stow. **2–5:** Photography Ian Gillet — **Jens Laugesen 2, 4, 9 & 10:** Photography Jens Laugesen Studio; model Camilla de la Moriniere. **3:** Photography Amy Troost; styling Alistair Mckimm; model Cristina Jurach @ SupremeModel. **5–8:** Photography catwalking.com. **11:** Photography Jean Francois Carly; model May Andersen @ 2PM — **Jolibe 1:** Sketch by Joel Diaz. **2 & 6:** Photography Christina LaPens. **3–5:** Photography Christina LaPens; styling Bernat Buscato — **Jonathan Saunders 1:** Still from Siobhan Davies' dance production, 'Endangered Species', photographed by Marije de Haas. **2:** Photography Clive Booth. **3–8:** Photography catwalking.com — **Kataryzna Szczotarska 1 & 4:** Photography catwalking.com. **2:** Photography Skye Parrot. **3 & 5:** Photography Geenie. **6–9:** Illustrations Kevin Tang — **Kosmetique Label 1 & 4–7:** Photography Alessandro Russino. **3, 8 & 9:** Photography Aito Kadama — **Laitinen 1:** Photography Shoji Fujii. **2, 4, 9 & 10:** Photography Chris Vidal; styling Tuomas Laitinen. **3:** Print design Escalier, created from Chris Vidal's photographs; image Lauri. **4:** Photography Chris Vidal; styling Tuomas Laitinen. **5–8:** Photography Chris Vidal; styling Jenny Jansson — **Louis de Gama 1:** Photography Rui Vasco; model Fiona @ Face Models. **2:** Photography Berndt Ottif. **3:** Photography Louis de Gama. **4:** Photography archive Moda Madeira; model Patricia Zhu @ Central Models. **5 & 7:** Photography archive Moda Madeira; model Barbara Tomasic @ Talia Models. **6:** Photography archive Moda Madeira; model Milene Veiga @ Central Models. **8 & 9:** Photography Andrew Hobbs — **Louise Amstrup** All photography Mads Perch; styling Jakob Brondum — **Lutz 1 & 7–9:** Photography David Ballu. **2:** Photography Petrov Ahner; **3, 4 & 6:** Photography Lutz. **5:** Photography Pascal Therme — **Manish Arora 1:** Photography Robert Astley Sparke; model Anna Kurzon @ Models 1. **3–6:** Photography Ian Gillett; styling Tamara Cincik. **7:** Photography Manish Arora — **Meadham/Kirchoff 1, 5 & 7:** Photography Nicolaj Moller. **2:** Photography Claire Robertson; styling Michael O Nybraten. **3:** Photography Thomas Giddings; styling Chloe Kerman. **4:** Photography Gabriella Massey. **6:** Photography Claire Robertson. **8:** Photography Thomas Giddings — **Miki Fukai 1, 3, 6 & 8:** Photography Philip Gay; styling Jodie Barnes; hair Stephen Low; makeup Sally Branka; model Melody; casting Thomas Jibogun. **2, 5 & 7:** Dennis Schoenberg; styling Jodie Barnes; hair Kazuya Matsumoto; makeup Natsumi Watanabe; model Portia; casting Thomas Jibogun. **4:** Photography Sean & Seng; styling Jodie Barnes; hair Adrian Clark; makeup Giovanna Cantone; model Isabel Neumair — **Mikio Sakabe** All photography Daniel Sannwald — **Modernist 1–4:** Photography Vanessa Ellis. **5:** Photography Andrew Jones — **Nasir Mazhar 1 & 3:** Photography Rafael Perez Evans. **2:** Photography Benjamin A Huseby; styling Thom Murphy; model Finbar — **Natalia Brilli** All photography Thomas Lillo; styling Eloïse Larochelle — **Nathan Jenden 1–4:** Photography catwalking.com. **5:** Illustration Nathan Jenden — **Olanic 1, 2, 5 & 7:** Photography Armando Ferrari. **3:** Print design Niki Taylor. **4:** Photography Nikki Taylor. **6:** Photography Anna Isola Crolla — **Osman Yousefzada** All photography Mitchel Sam. Illustration Osman Yousefzada — **Patrik Söderstam** All photography Patrik Söderstam — **Pelican Avenue 1:** Photography Hideki Iida. **2:** Video still by Pelican video. **3 & 4:** Photography Bettina Komenda; styling Priska Morger. **5 & 9:** Photography Shoji Fujii; styling Markus Strasser. **6 & 7:** Photography Tabasson Charaf; video still artwork Pelican video. **8:** Photography Dirk van Dosselaer — **Petar Petrov 1–3 & 5–8:** Photography Christoph Pirnbacher. **4:** Photography Raphael Just — **Peter Bertsch 1:** Photography Etienne Tordoir. **2:** Photography Ronald Stoops. **3:** Photograph courtesy of *Pulp* magazine. **4 & 6–9:** Photography Willy Cuylits. **5:** Photography Estelle Hanania — **Peter Pilotto 1 & 10:** Photography Etienne Tordoir. **2 & 3:** Photography Pieter Huybrechts & Ellen Smeets. **4:** Artwork Peter Pilotto. **5–8:** Photography Pieter Huybrechts & Ellen Smeets; styling Akiko Murata. **9:** Photography Mark Pillai; styling Robin Schulie — **Postweiler Hauber 1, 2 & 13:** Photography Rafa. **3, 4 & 14:** Photography Heinz Peter Knes. **5–12:** Photography Anne Cécile Noël. — **PPQ** Photography catwalking.com — **Pulver 1 & 4–8:** Photography Özgür Albayrak. **2 & 3:** Iris Janke — **Rad Hourani 1 & 2:** Photography Max Abadian; hair & makeup Marie Josée Galibert; model Ryan @ DNA. **3:** Photography Rad Hourani. Models Julia, Johanna, Heather, Darla, Agnes, Reid, Anna, Kat, Marla, Meghan, all from Mode Models — **Raeburn Design 1–3 & 7:** Photography Mike Blackett; model Lakiza @ fmmodelagency.com. **4:** Photography Mike Blackett; model Minna @ fmmodelagency.com. **5:** Sketch by Raeburn Design. **6:** Photography Mike Blackett; model Santina @ Next Models — **Richard Nicoll 1, 2 & 9:** Photography Philip Gay; styling Jacob K; model Ben Grimes. **4:** Illustration Richard Nicoll. **5–8:** Photography catwalking.com. **9:** Photography Jason Evans — **Robert Normand 1:** Photography Olivier Amsellem; artwork Emmanuelle Mafille. **2, 3 & 7:** Photography Catherine Servel. **4:** Artwork by Amélie Charroin. **5 & 6:** Photography Chris Plytas — **Romina Karamanea 1:** Photography Panos Davios. **2:** Photography Bill Georgoussis; model Olivia Dunin @ Independent. **3:** Photography Romina Karamanea. **4:** Photography Cleveland Aaron; hair Raphael Sally; makeup Linsey Alexander at MAC; model Zoe Zimmer @ Premier. **5:** Photography Panos Davios; hair & makeup Labros Faslis; model Sam Ostanevica. **6:** Photography Panos Davios. **7:** Photography Panos Davios; hair & makeup Labros Faslis; model Ortenca Aliaj — **Romy Smits 1, 3, 4, 5 & 6:** Photography Wanda Tuerlinkcx. **2:** Photography Godewijn Daled. All print designs, styling and art direction Romy Smits — **Rubecksen Yamanaka 1 & 2:** Photography Kent Baker; styling Felix Elisabetta Forma. **3 & 9:** Photography Kiyotaka Hatanaka; styling Felix Elisabetta Forma. **4–7:** Tomoko Nagakawa; styling Felix Elisabetta Forma — **Seïko Taki 1, 3–7 & 9:** Photography Yutaka Washima. **2 & 8:** Photography Kathy le Sant — **Siv Støldal 1 & 10:** Photography Siv Støldal. **2:** Photography catwalking.com; styling Thom Murphy. **3:** Photography Trine Guldager. **4:** Photography Lewis Ronald. **5–8:** Photography Scott Sandford; styling Siv Støldal. **9:** Photography Dennis Schoenberg. Styling Thom Murphy — **Slobodan Mihajlovic 1:** Photography Kumi. **2:** Photography Srdjan Stancic; model Filippo Cortini. **3:** Artwork Slobodan Mihajlovic for Roberto Cavalli. **4 & 5:** Photography Srdjan Stancic. **5 & 7:** Photography Vladimir Miladinovic; hair Marija; makeup Alexander Djikic; model Lady Tamara Bakic. T-shirt print collaboration with Jenny Mortsel — **Slow and Steady Wins the Race** All photographs and styling Slow and Steady Wins the Race — **Spijkers en Spijkers 1 & 3–6:** Photography Viviane Sassen; styling Spijkers en Spijkers. **2:** Photography Alique; styling Roel Schagen. **7:** Photography catwalking.com; styling Anthony Unwin. — **Steve J & Yoni P 1 & 7:** Photography Kashfihalford. **2 & 4:** Photography James Mountford; styling Darren Knight; hair Gow Tanaka; makeup Kim Brown; model Vladimir @ Premier. **3:** Photography Steve J & Yoni P. **5:** Photography James Mountford; styling Darren Knight; hair Gow Tanaka; makeup Kim Brown; model Gabriella @ Select. 6: Photography Sungjin Kim; styling Kevin Kim; hair Kuni; makeup Honda; model Emily @ Oxygen. **8:** Illustration Yoni Pai — **Swash 1 & 3–5:** Photography Johnny Barrington. **2:** Photography Shiro Katagiri. **6–9:** Photography Shoji Fujii; model Zora Star — **Telfar 1 & 8:** Photography Dom Smith. **3 & 9:** Photography Johnny Mischief. **4–7:** Photography Nina Mouritzen — **Tillmann Lauterbach 1, 2, 4 & 5:** Photography Richard Jensen. **3 & 7:** Photography Tillmann Lauterbach. **6:** Illustration Tillmann Lauterbach — **Tim Hamilton 1, 7 & 8:** Photography Tina Tyrell; styling Nico Klam. **2–6:** Photography Anraldo Anaya-Luca; styling Nico Klam — **Todd Lynn 1:** Photography Roger Deckker; fashion editor Sophia Niophitou; hair Gareth van Cuylenberg @ Streeters; makeup Sharon Dowsett @ CLM; model Kasia @ Women, Paris. **2:** US–Mexico boundary map from the Records of Boundary and Claims Commissions and Arbitrations, National Archives and Records Administration, College Park, Maryland. **3–6:** Photography catwalking.com. **7:** Photography Aitken Jolly; hair Martin Cullen @ Streeters; makeup Ozzy Salvatierra @ Streeters; model Sarah G @ Take Two. **8:** Artwork Todd Lynn — **Trosman 1, 3 & 4:** Photography Patricio Battellini. **2:** Photography Trosman. **5:** Photography Trosman. **6–8:** Photography David Dunan; styling Sebastian Kaufmann — **Txell Miras 1 & 8:** Photography Xavi Carmona. **2 & 3:** Photography Txell Miras. **5 & 7:** Photography Mirella Miras. **6:** Photography Josep Vila. **9:** Photography Ivan Caparròs — **Unconditional** All photography catwalking.com — **Ute Ploier 1–9:** Photography Bernd Preiml. **10:** Photography Shoji Fujii — **Yuko Yoashitake 1:** Photography Louis Girardi. **2:** Photography Anne-Marie Michel. **3:** Photography Ed Sykes. **4 & 5:** Prints Yuko Yoshitake. **6 & 7:** Photography Anon; styling Anna Clausen. **8:** Photography Anon. **9:** Photography Ben Kelaway; styling Lara Ferros. **Page 384:** Clothes by Frank Leder; photography Gregor Hohenberg.

Acknowledgments

Thank you to all the designers who gave their time to contribute to this book, and to their PRs who supported the project. A special thanks goes to Mandi Lennard, Michael Oliver-Salac at Blow PR and to Lulu Kennedy at Fashion East.

Thanks to Lee Widdows and Willie Walters at Central Saint Martins, Wendy Dagworthy at The Royal College of Art and to everyone at ITS in Trieste.

Many thanks to all the creatives, photographers, illustrators, stylists and models who provided fantastic imagery, time for interviews and an opportunity to witness their creativity.

A huge appreciation to everyone at Laurence King. Helen Evans, Lewis Gill and significantly Gaynor Sermon for keeping the project on track. Thanks also to Catherine Hooper for meticulous copy editing. A massive credit to byBOTH for brilliant art direction and to Lindsay May for keeping me organized.

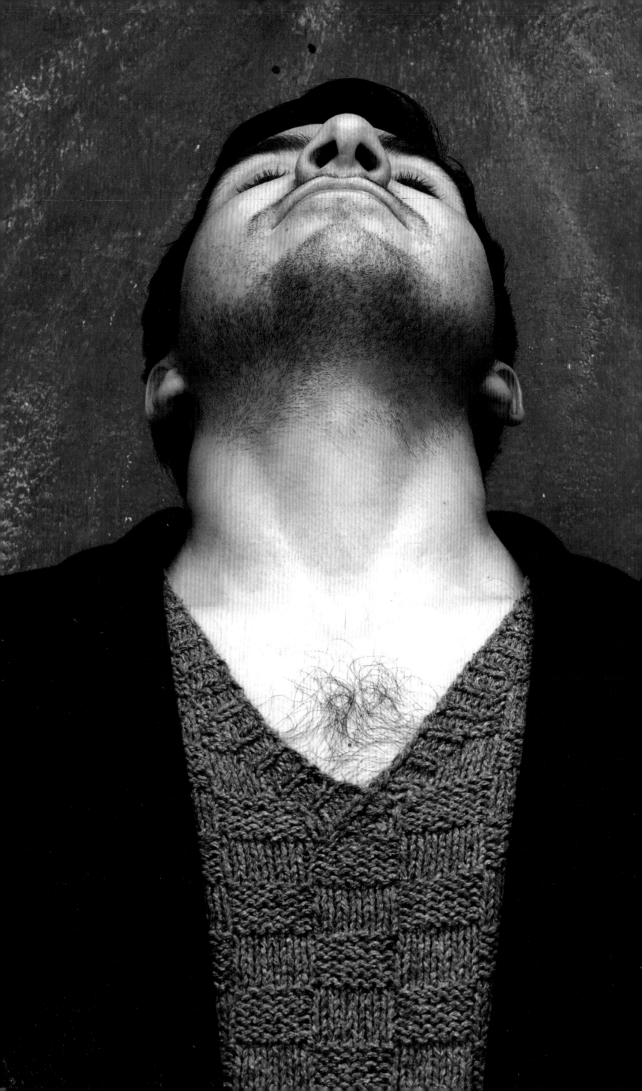